UNLEASHING THE HIDDEN POWER
of *Your*
Growing
Business

Scott A. Clark

Author of *Beating the Odds*

UNLEASHING THE HIDDEN POWER

of Your

Growing Business

amacom

American Management Association

New York • Atlanta • Boston • Chicago • Kansas City • San Francisco • Washington, D.C.
Brussels • Toronto • Mexico City

This book is available at a special
discount when ordered in bulk quantities.
For information, contact Special Sales Department,
AMACOM, a division of American Management Association,
135 West 50th Street, New York, NY 10020.

This publication is designed to provide accurate and authoritative
information in regard to the subject matter covered. It is sold with the
understanding that the publisher is not engaged in rendering legal,
accounting, or other professional service. If legal advice or other expert
assistance is required, the services of a competent professional person
should be sought.

Library of Congress Cataloging-in-Publication Data

Clark, Scott A.
    Unleashing the hidden power of your growing business / Scott A.
Clark.
        p.   cm.
    Includes bibliographical references and index.
    ISBN 0-8144-5001-6
    1. Organizational change.   2. Organizational effectiveness.
I. Title.
HD58.8.C523   1993
658.4'063—dc20   93-27889
                                                                         CIP

Printing number

10 9 8 7 6 5 4 3 2 1

Contents

Prologue

How to Get the Most From This Book

Just because you've launched your company and managed to achieve some real growth, there is no guarantee that your business will *continue* to be successful. Sustained success doesn't just happen; it requires a continuous, systematic effort on your part.

Macrofruition™ is a step-by-step program you can use to ensure that your company gets all the sustenance it needs to remain healthy and strong. By focusing on the key elements that underlie the success of any business, the Macrofruition process enables any company to keep growing and prospering no matter how stiff the competition.

During your company's journey to maturity, it will continue to undergo many changes. These changes are driven from without (by, for example, the economy or your industry), as well as from within (by management, employees, or your company size). If you accept the fact that your company is a dynamic, living entity, then you must also accept the fact that all parts of the company (including you) must undergo change if the business is to remain healthy and strong.

The Macrofruition process is designed to help you and your company weather these inevitable changes. Some of the steps are fairly easy. Others may be quite difficult. But the outcome of going fearlessly through the process—a stronger, more profitable company—is worth the effort. If you want to attain the height of success that your business is truly capable of achieving and if you want to separate your company from the myriad mediocre businesses out there, then Macrofruition is the process for you. If you are still a dreamer with a vision and fire in your soul and if you still have the willingness to make sacrifices to achieve great things with your business—even if it means altering your original plan—then I urge you to read on.

How to Get the Most out of This Book

If you try to complete the quest that lies before you merely by reading this book and then laying it down, you will have gained little. To get the most out of the book, you should approach it as a program to enhance your company. Work your way through it, applying the ideas and suggestions that are presented at every step of the way.

You'll find that ideas generated during one step will be enhanced by discoveries made within subsequent steps on your journey. None of the steps stands alone; all are interconnected.

You will see that I have placed critical exercises in boxes throughout the book. Their purpose is twofold: first, to get your creative juices flowing so you're ready for the next step; second, to help you begin building your own success foundation, brick by brick.

Without your notebook-and-pen participation, the exercises in this book will yield a level of understanding—the bricks—made of mental straw and unable to support anything of value. Therefore, I strongly suggest you arm yourself with a notebook in which to record your insights and to work through exercises so that your inspirational bricks will be constructed of solid granite.

Excellence can be attained if you . . .
Care more than others think is wise
Risk more than others think is safe
Dream more than others think is practical
Expect more than others think is possible.

—author unknown

Introduction

The Care and Feeding of a Healthy Business

Many company founders believe that, because they launched a successful business, they can count on its continued success without much further intervention. This is a dangerous misconception. All too often, after achieving a strong start and some measure of success, these misguided founders and CEOs stand by helplessly and watch their market share wither away, wondering what went wrong. In the worst cases, they lose their companies, and even their life savings, because of their failure to understand what was needed to keep their companies healthy and strong.

Your Potted Plant

Envision your business as a houseplant. To get your business to where it is today, you had to plant and nourish the seeds. But planting the seeds is not enough. You must continue to nurture your business if it is to remain healthy and strong.

Houseplants exist in three states: growing, stable, or dying. Likewise, your business has growth states. However, unlike a houseplant, an established business exists in one of only two possible states. It's either growing or dying. There's no such thing as a "stable" business; the company that stands still today is actually withering away while the world passes it by.

In this book we're going to focus on the ongoing nurturing required to get your business into full, dynamic bloom and to keep it there. We'll look at pruning a little here and there to keep your foliage lush and radiant. You'll learn about some innovative fertilizing techniques to keep your business growing strong. And you'll learn how to prevent and cure the many "failure viruses" to which companies are susceptible as they develop and mature.

Before we get started, I want you to be convinced that your company, like any other, is susceptible to failure no matter how strong and healthy it appears to be. Perhaps you believe that your product or service is so unique, your employees so competent, your managers so talented, that no failure virus could ever visit you. Maybe you are one of those confident executives who is certain nothing could happen that would seriously undermine the business. In case you are (and even if you are not), I want you to take out your notebook and do a little exercise.

Once you've completed this exercise, you should have a good idea of what internal and external factors could cause your company to fail. You can use this insight as a guide to help you identify the key problems you must address and resolve during your journey through these pages.

EXERCISE: Your Own Potential for Failure

Although the edifice of your company may appear sturdy, there are bound to be a number of structural weaknesses. Left unattended, these weaknesses can lead to the gradual demise or even the sudden collapse of your business—either from within (a disgruntled employee sabotages your computer system, for example) or because of external events (a competitor comes up with a product so superior that it jeopardizes your company's existence).

Open your notebook and create a section called "Failure Potential of My Company." I want you to envision and write down at least a dozen scenarios that could cause the demise of your company. I'll help you get started: Whatif you got hit by a Mack truck tomorrow and didn't recover? Could your business survive?

If you can't come up with at least a dozen probable failure scenarios for your company, you aren't much of a realist or planner, and the first attack against your establishment, whether from within or without, has the potential to reduce your productive business to a pile of rubble.

Now, try it again.

Macrofruition: The Ten-Step Process of Business Renewal

At this point you should be ready to accept the fact that a successful business requires proper nourishment and constant attention if it is to remain successful and achieve its true potential. One of the most effective ways to ensure that your company is getting the nourishment and attention it needs to flourish is to utilize a process called Macrofruition.

In the early 1970s I launched my first business. After several years and several spurts of growth, my company seemed to languish. It continued to experience periodic surges of growth, but the overall performance of the company had reached an apparent plateau.

In order to infuse my business with new vitality and to promote more predictable and continuous growth, I developed the Macrofruition program. Macrofruition is a ten-step process of business renewal (see Figure I-1) that focuses on the key elements that lead to sustained success for any business. By going through the process once a year, you will help to ensure that your company will continue to thrive, even in the midst of strong competition.

The order of the steps is deliberate and critical. The *basic* steps are first. You begin with an assessment of your present financial strength (Step One) and proceed to a new perspective on your business (Step Two). You next focus on maximizing your employee assets (Step Three) and rethinking your management philosophy (Step Four).

You then move on to the *advanced* steps, focusing on removing detrimental practices that can stymie company growth (Step Five) and developing new financial strategies in light of your progress thus far (Step Six). This section ends with a look at some ways to renovate your creative marketing tactics (Step Seven).

Finally, you are ready for the *strategic* steps, which involve three elements of effective strategic planning: the completion of an in-depth competitive analysis (Step Eight), the creation of a preliminary operating plan (Step Nine), and the development of a formal strategic business plan (Step Ten).

Strategic Avoidance

It could be argued that many of the activities within the Macrofruition process may have strategic consequences for your business. However, Steps Eight through Ten focus totally on strategic business initiatives

Figure I-1. The ten steps of Macrofruition.

STEP ONE
Complete Your Fiscal Check-up

STEP TWO
Shift Your Paradigms

STEP THREE
Build a Dedicated Employee Team

STEP FOUR
Rethink Your Management Philosophy

STEP FIVE
Remove Barriers and
Build Bridges to Profitability

STEP SIX
Increase Your Financial Savvy

STEP SEVEN
Expand Your Marketing Horizons

STEP EIGHT
Refine Your Competitive Wisdom

STEP NINE
Initiate a Team Planning Process

STEP TEN
Create Your Strategic Business Plan

involving longer-term activities and plans—efforts that will have a profound impact on the company's ability to survive in the future.

These strategic activities are overlooked or deemed unnecessary by many company executives; as a result, their businesses win some individual battles (secure customer orders) but still lose the war (go out of business). Unless you want your business to follow in their footsteps, I urge you to view all three parts of the Macrofruition process as being of equal importance.

One Step at a Time

Each of the steps of the Macrofruition process is explored in detail in the following chapters. Each step requires a significant effort and should be mastered to your complete satisfaction before you proceed to the next step, because there is an overall building process that is accomplished by the orderly completion of these steps.

By taking the Macrofruition journey step by step, resolving every issue as it arises, you will find that each subsequent step becomes far more productive. Although much data needs to be gathered and much energy expended along the way, I assure you that the effort is vital and the payback can be phenomenal.

A commitment to Macrofruition is by no means easy. It requires that you provide the specific nutrients your growing company needs, not just what you want to give it. Maintaining this ongoing commitment can prove to be difficult amid the ongoing demands and pressures of your business. But without such a commitment, although you may continue to see progress, you will never realize the true potential of your company.

In Step One, we begin the Macrofruition process, in which you assess the current state of your company's health. Through this financial examination, you pinpoint weaknesses or deficiencies that will be addressed as you proceed through the rest of the steps in the process.

Part I
The Basic Steps

Step One

Complete Your Fiscal Checkup

Any physician will tell you that before embarking on a strenuous new health regimen—which is what you'll be doing as you work your way through this book—it's a good idea to have a thorough checkup. Step One of the Macrofruition process is the equivalent of a medical checkup. It is a fiscal examination that focuses on key elements of past financial records to determine the state of your company's health.

But even before you proceed with the thorough examination you'll be conducting in Step One, you must check the pulse of your business to see if it's strong enough to weather the journey.

Check Your Business Pulse

As an astute business executive, with your finger on the pulse of your organization, you have a good idea of the general state of its health. You should be able to categorize your company as:

Green: Relatively healthy and able to sustain itself during the process of change outlined in these pages

Yellow: Some health problems, but generally able to sustain itself, provided you attend to relevant immediate problems, such as a needed capital infusion or a major marketing effort

Red: On the verge of collapse and in need of immediate sustained attention for survival

If you rated your company as Green, you can readily continue with the Macrofruition process. If you gave it a Yellow rating, you can proceed,

9

but you will need to attend to a few immediate problems concurrent with pursuing the Macrofruition process. However, if your rating was Red, you must attack the potentially fatal problems your company faces before proceeding with the Macrofruition program.[1]

Take the First Step

In Step One, you will examine all relevant financial data for your company for the past five years, focusing not just on the numbers, but especially on how those numbers vary over time. The idea is to spot significant trends—positive or negative—that will help you to pinpoint strengths and to identify weaknesses that must be overcome if your company is to remain successful.

Step One involves three distinct phases: data gathering, computation, and diagnosis. The data-gathering phase is easy, quick, and painless. It probably will involve analyzing fewer than twenty-five key items from your past financials; the most time-consuming part of the effort will be writing down the numbers. In the computational phase, you will convert the data you gathered in the first phase into meaningful information, such as percentages of sales and other financial ratios.

The diagnostic phase is the heart of Step One. In this phase, you will determine how key ratios vary over time and uncover potentially damaging trends so that corrective actions can be taken.

Before plunging into Phase 1, you should hold an executive staff meeting in which you brief key members of your management team, telling them that you are planning a number of specific initiatives intended to inject new vitality into the company and to strengthen its bottom line. The idea is to enlist the support of your key players in this effort and to assure them that they will be part of the ultimate decision-making process.

Phase 1: Gather the Data

Now it's time to begin gathering data. If you have an established, relatively stable company, gather your financial statements for the past five

1. For more information on turning around troubled companies, refer to a perspective developed by Charles "Red" Scott—a noted turnaround expert—in the article "Nine Steps to Save Troubled Companies" by John Banaszewski in *The Best of Inc. Guide to Business Strategy* (New York: Prentice-Hall Press, 1988), pages 47–52.

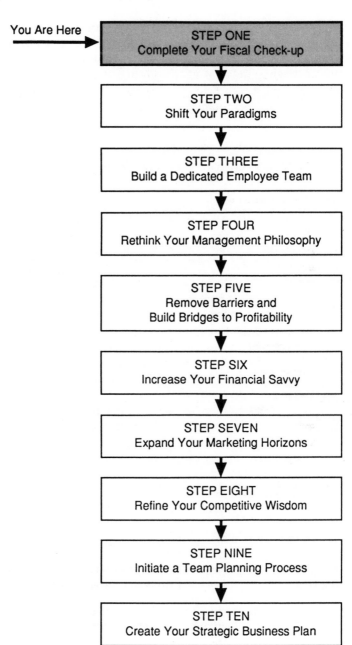

years. If your company experiences frequent hiccups or roller-coaster results (which is common for young companies), you may also want to include a monthly analysis covering the past two years so that you can review precisely when the peaks and valleys occurred.

If you have almost completed your current fiscal year, I suggest you generate a set of pro forma financials for this year as well to factor into the equation.

Figure 1-1. Selected critical business data–historical worksheet format.

Section A. Data from annual income statement.

	5 Years Ago	4 Years Ago	3 Years Ago	2 Years Ago	1 Year Ago
Sales					
Cost of sales					
Labor expenses					
Material expenses					
Selling expenses					
Gross profit					
Engineering department expenses†					
Admin. department expenses†					
Mktng. department expenses†					
Additional department expenses†					
Other overhead expenses†					
Total operating expenses					
Operating profit (EBIT)*					
Net profit					

*Operating profit is also referred to as earnings before interest and taxes, or EBIT.

Section B. Data from annual balance sheet.

	5 Years Ago	4 Years Ago	3 Years Ago	2 Years Ago	1 Year Ago
Accounts receivable					
Current assets					
Inventory					
Fixed assets					
Total assets					
Current liabilities					
Total liabilities					
Retained earnings					
Total equity					

Figure 1-1 illustrates a form you can use to gather your data. I have included on the form items I would deem essential if I were to analyze a business. You may have some additional items that you consider relevant; these should be added to your list. In gathering the data, try to plug any holes with realistic estimates.

Data from past company income statements are gathered in Section A of Figure 1-1. I recommend breaking the Cost of Sales (in the top portion of Section A) into three basic components: *Labor Expenses*—the labor required to build your product—which may be omitted for a service, distribution, or retail business; *Material Expenses*—the costs of the material needed to produce your product or service; and *Selling Expenses*—the direct selling costs associated with closing the order.

If your company has a number of different departments, I suggest you break out the expenses by department, as I've done (note the entries marked with daggers in Section A of Figure 1-1), so that you can track changes in the relationship between departmental expenses and sales over the past five years.[2] This will give you a clearer picture of where the money is spent and may help you uncover hidden problems or worrisome trends. The term *Other Overhead Expenses* refers to the balance of the operating expenses, such as the cost of rent, telephone, and legal and accounting services.

Section B includes key data extracted from past company balance sheets.

As an example, in Figure 1-2 I've recorded data from an actual company, which I'll call Acme Company. This is an established manufacturing business with continuously increasing sales.

Phase 2: Compute the Critical Ratios

Once you have gathered the data, you must transform them into meaningful information that will help you guide the business. First, convert your income statement data (from Section A of Figure 1-2) into percentage of sales figures, as shown in the Acme Company example (Section C of Figure 1-3). To do this, simply divide each piece of data by the total sales for that particular period. (A spreadsheet program for your computer can make Phases 2 and 3 practically painless.) By expressing all the income statement data as a percentage of a common value (sales) that symbolizes

---

2. If you have a manufacturing business, note that Production Department Expense is recorded as the labor portion of Cost of Sales.

Figure 1-2. Selected critical business data–historical worksheet example (figures in $000).

Section A. Acme Company: annual income statement data.

	5 Years Ago	4 Years Ago	3 Years Ago	2 Years Ago	1 Year Ago
Sales	260	680	3,710	6,680	8,390
Cost of sales	100	400	2,110	3,580	4,540
Labor expenses	50	200	1,050	1,790	2,170
Material expenses	40	165	660	1,100	1,400
Selling expenses	10	35	400	690	970
Gross profit	160	280	1,600	3,100	3,850
Engineering department expenses	40	60	150	300	390
Admin. department expenses	80	195	320	510	680
Mktng. department expenses	0	101	160	300	490
Additional department expenses	0	0	0	0	0
Other overhead expenses	250	554	770	1,350	1,350
Total operating expenses	370	910	1,400	2,460	2,910
Operating profit (EBIT)	(210)	(630)	200	640	940
Net profit	(210)	(610)	200	620	910

Section B. Acme Company: annual balance sheet data.

	5 Years Ago	4 Years Ago	3 Years Ago	2 Years Ago	1 Year Ago
Accounts receivable	20	150	820	1,320	1,450
Current assets	330	580	1,550	2,740	2,920
Inventory	200	430	700	1,420	1,360
Fixed assets	70	120	130	240	260
Total assets	410	730	1,660	2,970	3,120
Current liabilities	20	330	1,010	1,290	1,950
Total liabilities	580	1,110	1,700	2,960	3,100
Retained earnings	(910)	(1,520)	(1,320)	(700)	210
Total equity	(170)	(380)	(40)	10	20

company growth, the subsequent analysis becomes far easier to accomplish, as you shall see.

Next, continuing with the Acme example, use the balance sheet data (from Section B of Figure 1-2) to compute some common (and not-so-common) ratios:

Liquidity

First, focus on the liquidity of your business, i.e., on how readily its assets can be converted into cash. There are two important ratios to compute. The first is the *current ratio*, defined as:

$$\frac{\text{Current assets}}{\text{Current liabilities}}$$

The larger this ratio, the better the position of your debt financiers, the greater their safety net, and the more cash you have to cover unforeseen contingencies. On the other hand, a number that is too large indicates poor cash management (idle cash, excessive inventories, or poor credit management). Financiers usually consider a ratio of 2:1 to be optimum for most businesses.

As an example, if your company has current assets of $500,000 and current liabilities of $250,000 (for a current ratio of 2:1), financiers will perceive that the company can pay off all its debts and still have an additional $250,000 in assets, a reasonable safety factor.

A more stringent test is the *quick ratio* (also called the *acid-test ratio*). This ratio excludes inventories from your current assets, since they may prove difficult to turn into cash in an emergency. The resultant figure (current assets minus inventories) is referred to as *quick assets*. The quick ratio is computed as follows:

$$\frac{\text{Quick assets}}{\text{Current liabilities}}$$

Financiers like to see a quick ratio between 1.0 and 2.0, meaning that current assets are at least as great as current liabilities. However, the more risk they perceive your business to have, the higher they will want this ratio to be.

Suppose your company has a quick ratio of 1.6, with $320,000 in quick assets and $200,000 in current liabilities. In an emergency, the company would be able to pay off current debt and still have $120,000 remaining for operations. This is probably satisfactory for a relatively low-risk operation.

If either of these ratios is too low relative to the norm in your industry (as covered in the discussion of the *RMA Annual Statement Studies* later in this chapter), you might consider one or more of the following remedies:

Pay off some debts; restructure some short-term debt (payable within the next year) into long-term debt (payable beyond the next year); increase your current assets with a new infusion of equity; or plow some profits back into the business. If you need to improve the quick ratio, also try to reduce inventories substantially, possibly by selling or writing off obsolete material.

Leverage

Next, look at leverage, which is simply a measure of the degree of debt financing your company has. The relevant figure is the *debt-to-assets ratio*, computed as follows:

$$\frac{\text{Total liabilities}}{\text{Total assets}}$$

This number should be expressed as a percentage. Bankers want to see this number considerably lower than 100 percent, because they want to be certain you have enough assets to pay off all your debt (including their loans). The higher this percentage, the greater the risk that you will be unable to meet your debt payments.

Equity investors, on the other hand, want to see a higher percentage so that you can maximize leverage and thus make the most money for them. To boost this ratio, they may, for example, require that you lease your capital equipment rather than buy it.

Suppose your company has total liabilities of $1.5 million and total assets of $1.8 million; the company's debt-to-assets ratio is 83 percent. This will make bankers very nervous, and they will probably insist you infuse more equity into the company (or reduce the debt) before lending you additional funds.

Asset Management

One of a CEO's most important financial duties is to keep the assets of the business working hard and productively. If your inventories are larger than needed or your accounts receivable are longer than they should be, you are doing a poor job in this department.

If your company is involved in manufacturing, distribution, or retail sales, you should track *inventory turns*, which measures how rapidly you are rotating, or turning over, your inventory. Although there are several ways to compute this figure, one commonly used equation is:

$$\frac{\text{Cost of sales}}{\text{Average inventory}}$$

where average inventory is defined as:

$$\frac{(\text{Inventory at end of } \textit{previous} \text{ period} - \text{inventory at end of } \textit{current} \text{ period})}{2}$$

The more times you rotate your inventory each year, the less money you have tied up in inventory and the more you have available for other uses. The lower your typical profit margins, the higher this number should be, because dormant inventory eats up profits. Although a company that sells high-ticket items (such as road graders) may rotate inventory only once or twice a year, most other businesses should aim for higher turnover; while an inventory turns figure of 4 may be good, a figure of 12 could be great.

As an example, if the value of your inventory was $800,000 at the end of the previous year and is $1.3 million at the end of the current year, your average inventory is $1.05 million. If your cost of sales is $1.89 million for the same period, you will have rotated your inventory only 1.8 turns during the year. Assuming your company does not sell high-ticket items, your financiers will perceive this to be a pitifully low number and an indication of poor asset management because of the additional costs associated with maintaining this slow-moving inventory.

If you allow your customers to buy on credit, you should compute *accounts receivable aging*. Although the historical data needed to reconstruct this number for past years may not exist, you can calculate a close approximation as follows:

First, compute *daily sales* (for the year), which equals:

$$\frac{\text{Net sales}}{360}$$

Then, your *accounts receivable aging* can be approximated by:

$$\frac{\text{Accounts receivable}}{\text{Daily sales}}$$

This calculation gives you an approximation of the average length of time you are carrying your receivables. Try to achieve thirty days, but anything over forty-five days is a crime.

Consider this example: Suppose your annual sales are $4.5 million. Your daily sales are then $12,500. If your accounts receivable at year's end is $860,000, your accounts receivable aging is almost sixty-nine days. This is horrible. If you are currently borrowing money at 15 percent, you have the potential to realize a free cash infusion of $300,000 by reducing your aging to forty-five days.

Profitability

Shareholders and investors are naturally interested in financial ratios that relate to profits. I recommend tracking two key ratios here, both of which should be expressed as a percentage.

The first ratio, *return on assets* (ROA), is a measure of how well you have utilized the assets of the company to generate a profit. It is computed as follows:

$$\frac{\text{Net profit}}{\text{Total assets}}$$

If your company realized a net profit of $250,000 and had total assets of $750,000, you would have an ROA of 33 percent, a respectable number.

The second ratio, *return on equity* (ROE), is of interest to equity investors. ROE, also referred to as *return on net worth*, measures how well you are managing their investment so as to maximize their profits. ROE is computed as follows:

$$\frac{\text{Net profit}}{\text{Equity}}$$

If your company closes the year with a net profit of $250,000 and has total equity of $400,000, your ROE is 63 percent, again a respectable number. A caution here, however. If you have too little equity in a rapidly growing company, the ROE can exceed 1,000 percent (as in Section D of Figure 1-3). This indicates, not incredible performance, but rather an incredible lack of equity. In addition, if both equity and net profit are negative, this number is meaningless (observe the "N/A" in Section D of Figure 1-3).

Figure 1-3. Selected critical business data–key historical measures.

Section C. Key measures expressed as a percentage of sales (computed from income statement data).

	5 Years Ago	4 Years Ago	3 Years Ago	2 Years Ago	1 Year Ago	Targets
Cost of sales (%)	38	59	57	54	54	50
Production department expenses (%)	19	29	28	27	26	20
Gross profit (%)	62	41	43	46	46	50
Engineering department expenses (%)	15	9	4	4	5	4
Admin. department expenses (%)	31	29	9	8	8	8
Mktng. department expense (%)	0	15	4	4	6	8
Additional department expenses (%)	-	-	-	-	-	-
Total operating expenses (%)	142	134	38	37	35	35
Operating profit (%)	-81	-93	5	10	11	15
Net profit (%)	-81	-90	5	9	11	10

Section D. Key business ratios (computed primarily from balance sheet data).

	5 Years Ago	4 Years Ago	3 Years Ago	2 Years Ago	1 Year Ago	Targets
Current ratio	16.50	1.76	1.53	2.12	1.50	2:1
Quick ratio	0.22	0.14	0.50	0.45	0.50	1.5:1
Debt-to-assets ratio (%)	141	152	102	100	99	60
Inventory turns	0.51	1.27	3.73	3.38	3.27	6 turns
Accounts receivable aging	27.69	79.41	79.57	71.14	62.22	45 days
Return on assets (%)	-51	-84	12	21	29	30
Return on equity (%)	N/A	N/A	-500	6,200	4,500	25
Z-score	-6.03	-10.70	0.33	3.89	4.29	+4.0

The Z-Score

The Z-score was developed in the mid-1960s by Edward Altman.[3] Although it was originally developed to measure the likelihood of bankruptcy, the Z-score has proved over time to be an excellent measure of the overall financial health of a company.[4]

The Z-score can be used to spot danger signals before they lead to major catastrophes. If a company's Z-score is less than 1.1, bankruptcy is

3. As detailed in Edward I. Altman, *Corporate Financial Distress* (New York: Wiley, 1983).
4. Resist the temptation to use only the Z-score as a measure of your success, because your financiers will use the other ratios and you need to satisfy those as well.

probably looming. If a company's score is above 2.6, the business is on solid ground.[5]

Although the absolute value of your company's Z-score is always relevant, it is most important for this step in the Macrofruition process to focus on how your Z-score varies over time. No matter what the size of your company, no matter what its stage of growth, the relative change in your company's Z-score over time provides a reliable measure of how well your company is doing and of the direction in which it's headed.

The power of the Z-score lies in the fact that it incorporates a number of key factors that affect your financial health and weighs them according to their importance. The formula for the Z-score considers profits as good, assets as marginally beneficial, long-term liabilities as bad, and current liabilities as horrible.

The Z-score is computed in steps, starting with the calculation of four ratios:

X_1, which is a measure of your company's liquidity, is computed as follows:

$$\frac{(\text{Current assets} - \text{current liabilities})}{\text{Total assets}}$$

X_2, which measures your company's cumulative profitability over time (if a company has been profitable and then begins to lose money, this ratio will start to fall), is calculated as follows:

$$\frac{\text{Retained earnings}}{\text{Total assets}}$$

X_3, a measure of return on assets, equals

$$\frac{\text{Operating profit}^6}{\text{Total assets}}$$

X_4, the inverse of the debt-to-equity ratio:

$$\frac{\text{Net worth}}{\text{Total liabilities}}$$

5. As determined from Altman's studies.
6. Operating profit is also referred to as earnings before interest and taxes, or EBIT.

Once you have calculated these four ratios, simply plug them into the Z-score formula:

$$\text{Z-score} = 6.56(X_1) + 3.26(X_2) + 6.72(X_3) + 1.05(X_4)$$

Early-stage and surging growth companies may have negative Z-scores (because their X_2, X_3, and/or X_4 values may be negative), whereas established profitable companies usually have positive Z-scores. But in all cases, the incremental changes in your company's Z-score over time should be positive. If your Z-score starts to fall sharply over several accounting periods, warning bells should ring.

The Ideal Values

Appropriate target goals for the eight key measurements we've just calculated vary, depending on your industry and on other factors, such as the size, age, and location of your company. If you don't already have a handle on the typical values for your business, you'd better learn them fast, because chances are your financiers are already comparing your company's performance against their estimates of what these values should be.

To develop a set of ideal target values for your company, first talk to your accountant. Then visit your financiers (both debt and equity) to get their input. Ask to borrow the latest copy of the *RMA (Robert Morris Associates) Annual Statement Studies*, the financier's bible for these ratios.[7] This reference shows typical ratios by industry and will give you a clear idea of where you should be in order to perform on a par with your industry peers.

Using all this input, you can develop a clear set of target values for your business. To avoid the halo effect (the tendency to make your data agree with the goals you have established), you should determine these target values *before* computing your company's actual ratios.

If some of the targets you develop are better than industry standards, great. But if some of them are worse, you had better have a valid reason, because your financiers will challenge any targets that are less than your industry standard.

Once you have arrived at your target values, record them in the "Target" column of your version of Figure 1-3.

---

7. Larger libraries may have the book as well. If you want your own copy, you can order it from Robert Morris Associates, One Liberty Place, Philadelphia, Penn. 19103.

EXERCISE: Your Company's Tire Tracks

Now it's time to calculate the actual results achieved by your company and see how they compare with the targets you've set. The key to this exercise is not the numbers themselves, but the trends they suggest. The important question to ask is whether the numbers are heading in the direction of your target values.

Generate two sets of tables in your notebook, the first one similar to Figure 1-2 (in which you record your raw data) and the second similar to Figure 1-3 (in which you record your calculated results). Add a column to each table in which to record the estimated results for your current fiscal year, which will give you a more immediate perspective of your company's trends.

As you set up your tables, add any additional data lines, ratios, and percentages that are uniquely applicable to your business, provided you have some control over them (there's no point in tracking items you can't do anything about). For example, if you sell via direct mail or retail, you may want to review your advertising cost as a percentage of sales. If you have a service company, you may want to track transportation costs as a percentage of sales.

Remember, these data represent history. You can't change the past. However, to paraphrase Santayana, those who don't understand the business mistakes of their past are condemned to repeat them. So you had best develop a clear understanding of your company's past performance if you hope to improve it.

Please resist the temptation to claim that you already know your company's shortcomings and thereby don't see the need to write down what you already know. Our journey through these pages will cause you to view your company from many perspectives; without planting these written seedlings now, you won't be able to see the forest for the trees later.

Phase 3: Diagnose Financial Diseases

Now that you've calculated the key performance ratios for your company, it's time to enter the diagnostic phase of the fiscal checkup. When you've examined your financial statements in the past, you probably focused on the actual values of each item. Now I want you to concentrate on the changes in key measures and ratios from the first period to the last period of the results table (see Figure 1-3).

Study each line in your version of Figure 1-3. As you do so, ask yourself the following questions:

- How are the values changing over time? Is there little or no change? Are values changing slowly? Rapidly?
- Is this the rate of change you want? If not, what can you do to achieve the desired rate of change?
- Are the values relatively stable, or are they fluctuating randomly—or wildly—over time? Why or why not?
- Are the values advancing toward or retreating from the targets you previously established? Why or why not? If they are moving away from your targets, what can you do to get them headed in the right direction?

Orderly Results

If your values, and their trends over time, compare favorably with the targets you established, you (and your financiers) should be pleased. Your application of the Macrofruition program should make these good results even better.

If your current values are orderly but their direction or rates of change cause you concern, look at the components of the key ratios in question to ascertain what corrective action you need to take. For example, if your debt-to-asset ratio is too high, you might consider either decreasing liabilities (by paying off debts or converting debt to equity) or increasing your assets (by bettering profits or raising additional equity).

Disorderly Results

Are your values shooting rapidly up and down without any discernible trend? If so, this is a dangerous situation, one that requires immediate attention. For excellent advice on what to do, refer to the article, "Nine Steps to Save Troubled Companies," mentioned in the first footnote in this chapter.

If your values show quite a bit of fluctuation over time, it might be helpful to go back and recalculate the data, using monthly rather than yearly financial statements. By smoothing the data in this way, you should get a clearer picture of underlying trends.

The Acme Company Fiscal Checkup

Now it's time to look more closely at the numbers you calculated. To guide you in analyzing your own company results, I'm going to walk you through my analysis of the Acme Company figures.

My Analysis

As I review the results for the Acme Company, I perceive that the business is generally in good shape. From Figure 1-2, I see that the business is experiencing both continued growth in sales and solid gross profits.

Figure 1-3 shows that operating expenses are generally in line with the target but that a continued reduction of production expenses needs to be pursued to meet the 20 percent target for that item. Except for return on equity, which is fluctuating wildly, the results seem to be orderly.

Inventory seems higher than warranted, as measured by the below-target inventory turns figures. The owner should investigate whether the company has too much obsolete inventory or whether stocking levels are too high. Accounts receivable aging is trending down but is still a problem, necessitating an analysis of the cause (is it Acme's general policy, or are a few major customers the culprits?).

EXERCISE: Laying the Groundwork for Improvement

Now that you've seen the autopsy of Acme's past five years, as well as an assessment of the corrective action that's needed, it's time to turn the spotlight on your company again.

Prepare an analysis in your notebook that details the potential problems you face, and include the most probable solutions to these problems. You may want to solicit the assistance of your banker and your CPA, but only after you have completed your initial critique of your results. Leave space at the conclusion of your entry for the additional perspectives of these two outside sources.

At the completion of your analysis, prepare a list of all the potential corrective actions that you considered from your analysis of all the key ratios. In this way you can spot certain steps you can take that will positively affect several critical ratios simultaneously. These are the activities to pursue first, since they can rapidly improve the health of the company.

The current ratio is below the target level, as is the quick ratio, indicating a potential liquidity problem. The biggest red flag is the debt-to-assets ratio, which is far too high and which has gone down very little over the past three years.

Although there can be multiple causes for the deficiencies in these three ratios (current, quick, and debt-to-assets) if they occur individually, the fact that all three are inadequate strongly suggests that the Acme Company has far too much debt and not enough equity. Acme probably needs to convert some owner's debt into equity, in addition to raising additional equity, in order to receive any additional bank loans.

This conclusion is further substantiated by the astronomically high return on equity. The figure is high, not because the company is in good shape, but because the company's current equity is far too small. Accordingly, the company needs a sizable infusion of additional equity (or a conversion of debt to equity).

Figure 1-4. Summary of financial corrective actions.

Topic	Definition	Key Measures	How to Improve
Liquidity	How readily company assets can be converted into cash	Current ratio Quick ratio	• Increase current assets. • Decrease current liabilities. • Eliminate problem inventories.
Leverage	Measure of a company's degree of debt financing	Debt-to-assets ratio	• Decrease total liabilities. • Increase total assets.
Asset management	Measure of productive use of company assets	Inventory turns Accounts receivable aging	• Decrease inventories. • Decrease receivables aging.
Profitability	Commitment of assets and equity to generate profits	Return on assets Return on equity	• Increase net profit. • Reduce operating expenses.
Z-score	Measure of overall company health	Z-score	• Maximize net profit. • Decrease fixed assets. • Increase current assets. • Decrease current liabilities.

Detrimental factors should always be reviewed together. Correcting one deficiency will probably affect others positively as well. In the case of Acme, an infusion of equity would improve the current ratio, the quick ratio, and the debt-to-assets ratio simultaneously.

To assist you in this process, Figure 1-4 presents a summary of the various corrective actions in a format that lets you see the interrelationships.

*   *   *

In Step One, you verified the known strengths and deficiencies of your company and probably uncovered some new ones as well. The insight you have gained will serve as a beacon to illuminate each subsequent step along the Macrofruition path.

In Step Two we examine the importance of paradigms to the sustained success of a business. It's not uncommon for two businesses in similar industries, appropriately capitalized and led by two highly capable management teams and launched at the same time, to meet with very different fates. When one company fails and a similar one succeeds, the winner is likely to be the one whose executives recognized and shifted their own paradigms to stay one step ahead of the competition—the focus of Step Two.

Step Two
Shift Your Paradigms

Without frequent infusions of new ideas and energy, businesses invariably find that their profits reach a plateau, then decline. As a result, many businesses that were once perceived as competitive tigers have become little more than plodding elephants. Step Two of Macrofruition describes a process you can apply to infuse new life into your business, even if it is a profitable one, by expanding your vision to encompass new products and/or new markets.

The Paradigm Trap

Every so often, a new buzzword comes along that is hyped by the business community without a real understanding of what it's all about. *Empowerment* and *excellence* fall into this category. So does *paradigm*, the corporate buzzword of the hour.

In Step Two, you will be introduced to the concept of paradigms. You will learn how to identify your own strongly held business paradigms, some of which may be preventing your company from realizing its true potential. More important, you will begin to develop new, more powerful paradigms that will help your business achieve a higher level of success.

Although the concept of paradigms has been around for decades, it has gained widespread public attention only in recent years. In his classic 1962 book *The Structure of Scientific Revolutions*, Thomas Kuhn provided the first major contemporary discussion of the paradigm concept as it applied to science. In the 1980s, business futurist Joel Barker took the

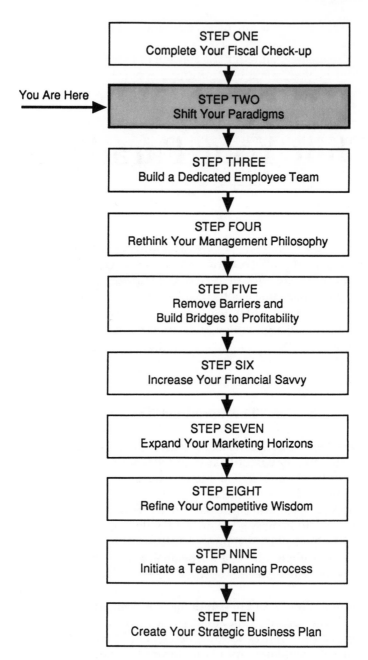

concept out of the realm of science and applied it to the world of business.[1]

Unfortunately, although the concept of paradigms has been eagerly embraced by young and old executives espousing change, many of its promoters never really understood the true meaning and power of the term.

The dictionary defines a paradigm as "a pattern or a model." Paradigms are the rules and regulations, often unconscious, that people apply as they go through the motions of daily living. The way people view the world, and the way they act in it, is governed by their paradigms. For example, paradigms determine whether you see the world as hostile or friendly, which church you attend or whether you attend at all, how you view poor and wealthy people, whether you're a Democrat, a Republican, or neither.

As people's everyday lives are governed by a vast set of paradigms, so, too, their business lives are governed by a host of paradigms that dictate such things as how they sell their products, how they deal with customers, how they treat employees, how they advertise, how they organize their financials, and the way they create new products and services.

There's nothing wrong with paradigms. They help people make sense of the world. The problem arises when people fail to recognize the paradigms that drive them and close their minds to the possibilities of other, more useful paradigms.

People are constantly exposed to a wealth of data from the world around them. But they don't take it all in. Paradigms act as filters that unconsciously screen the data, causing people to accept certain data—those that agree with their paradigms—and discard the rest.

This tendency to filter data according to paradigms is called the *paradigm effect*. Here's an example of how it works:

Suppose I told you a story of how a father and his young son left home in the family automobile to go on a fishing trip. While en route to the fishing lodge, the father was killed and the boy critically injured in an automobile accident. The son was rushed to a hospital and prepared for surgery. The surgeon walked into the operating room, took one look at

1. Several of the concepts presented in this chapter have been adapted from Joel Barker, *Future Edge: Discovering the New Paradigms for Success* (New York: Morrow, 1992). I heartily recommend that this book be required reading for everyone in your company.

the boy lying on the table, and shouted, "I can't operate on him; he's my son!" How could this be?

If you were confused by this story, one of your paradigms got in the way. Your paradigm indicated that surgeons are male, when in fact this surgeon was the boy's mother. Paradigms, by the way, are nothing more than a form of prejudice, or "pre-judging."

The Business of Paradigms

The paradigm effect can have serious consequences for people's business lives, blinding them to opportunities right before their eyes. Consider these hypothetical examples:

• A scientist employed by a pharmaceutical company ignores unexpected and seemingly invalid data from an experiment and thereby misses the opportunity to discover a powerful new painkiller, which a rival company discovers years later.

• A businessman overlooks the possibility that his metal-detecting widget for cereal boxes (a decidedly small market) could just as easily be used as a vehicle detector for home and business driveways (a decidedly larger market).

• An enterpreneur fails to realize that the instrument her company designed for military aircraft has an even bigger market—the commercial aircraft industry.

The Dangers of Clinging to Paradigms

It's easy to get stuck in a paradigm—especially if your paradigms have led to success in the past. The trouble is, those same paradigms that made you successful in the past may be preventing you from anticipating the future, leaving you vulnerable to competitors who *are* looking ahead.

The history of business is filled with examples of inventions spawned by paradigm shifts. Some—like 3M's Post-it notes and the Sony Walkman—were small. Others—for example, the development of airplanes, transistor radios, television, nuclear energy, lasers, photocopiers, and instant cameras, and the shift from mechanical to electronic watches—were major innovations. Whether large or small, all were the result of people breaking out of the mental molds of the past (and in many cases bucking the tides of naysayers who discouraged them).

A departure from a previously embraced paradigm involves risk, and most people don't care for that. But especially in today's highly competitive global world, there's even more risk in clinging to old paradigms. If you are not continually looking for new paradigms, you can bet your competitors are. (Remember how Ted Turner's competitors laughed when he proposed a twenty-four-hour cable news network? They're not laughing anymore.)

A failure to act does not protect you, because paradigms *will* shift, with or without you. And when a paradigm shifts, your business goes back to zero; your past successes guarantee absolutely nothing. If you cling to your paradigm and your competitor discovers a new, more powerful paradigm, you could quickly find yourself in the position of the Swiss watchmakers, whose business was wiped out virtually overnight when electronic watches were introduced.

The bigger and more established the organization, the more difficult the paradigm shift will be, in part due to bureaucracy, in part due to the complacency (and in some cases, arrogance) that comes with size. IBM is a good example. IBM's total computer market focus was on manufacturing and selling business computers to major corporations. Then along came a young upstart—Apple Computer—with a new paradigm that resulted in a line of computers for home and small-business use. IBM scoffed at the trivial company, the trivial idea, and the trivial market. Belatedly, Big Blue is scrambling to catch up.

All of us are presented with opportunities to reap the benefits of shifted paradigms. All we have to do is keep our minds open to new possibilities.

A paradigm shift I made while working in my first start-up company resulted in a highly successful product. The company manufactured monitoring systems for business and agriculture. As rural crime began to skyrocket, we recognized a need for a driveway monitor for farmsteads and starting thinking about developing one.

The monitor would have to be inexpensive and reliable. Conventional photocell or infrared units weren't the answer, because they would also be set off by the farmer's dogs and children. We'd have to come up with a better alternative.

First, we tried a buried pressure switch. This worked for a while, but the coarse gravel of the farm driveways gradually chewed up the switch. If we tried to protect the switch, then it wouldn't sense the vehicles.

Next we tried the buried wire loop that traffic signals utilize to activate left-turn lane arrows. These worked fine until the ground got wet and shorted out the loop (city loops encased in concrete didn't suffer this malady, but few farm driveways were made of concrete). So we were back to square one—until we experienced our paradigm shift.

I had spent years working in the space program, and now I recalled the search-coil magnetometers we had designed to measure the strength of the earth's magnetic field in space. I reasoned that a moving metal car would temporarily alter the earth's magnetic field in the vicinity of the farm driveway. Therefore, an alarm system based on magnetometers might be the solution we were searching for.

We converted the space program design into a small, inexpensive probe that could be buried next to the farm driveway to detect moving metal. The system, Farm Sentry, was a smashing success.

If you look behind the most successful businesses, you'll find that they thrive on shifting paradigms, doing things differently, defying conventional wisdom. One favorite example of mine is Swanson Chrysler-Plymouth, a car dealership in St. Petersburg, Florida. General manager George Fischell wanted to reverse the trend of sinking car sales. He surveyed his customers and found that what people hate the most about buying cars is dickering over the price. He decided to shift the industry paradigm by firing all his salespeople and putting rock-bottom prices—the best deal he was willing to give customers—on all cars in his lot. No more used car salesmen, no more haggling. The result: New car sales skyrocketed at Fischell's dealership, despite the predictions of some industry critics who "knew" this innovative dealer would fall on his face.

Identifying Paradigm Shifters

Any aspect of your business might be ripe for a paradigm shift, if only you take the time to discover the possibilities. Never forget that your present paradigms, essential as they are, may be preventing you from making a breakthrough that will carry your business to new heights.

Who within your company will generate new paradigms? Some company executives believe that practical new directions for the company (which is what paradigms represent, after all) can come only from staff members with long tenure, people who know and understand the company system and the rules. In fact, these are the very people who usually cling the most tenaciously to old paradigms. Betting the future on these folks is like expecting to be led out of a maze by three blind mice—it just won't happen.

It is my observation that the key people in any company come in four flavors:

First there is the *champion of the status quo*, a traditionalist who fervently embraces present paradigms. He or she absolutely will not change. Don't look to these employees if you want to find new ways of doing business.

The second type of employee is the *camp follower*. This person's primary objective is not to rock the boat. He or she will always side with the majority (or the boss). If you can convince the majority (or at least the camp follower's boss) to change, you may have a chance to win over this employee to the idea of a paradigm shift.

Third, there is the *adaptor*, the person who is open to change that can be justified as beneficial for the company. Unlike the camp follower, the adaptor is at least a somewhat independent thinker. This person may not actively search for new paradigms, but he or she will be open to them, if they seem to have potential.

Fourth, there is the *innovator*, who is never satisfied with the status quo, who is constantly driven to look for a better way of doing things. *This is usually the person who provides the seeds that germinate into paradigm shifts.* Unfortunately, this employee is frequently ostracized by most corporations, when he or she should be embraced as the company psychic.

Try to assign every one of your key employees to one of these categories, to help you focus on where your company's paradigm shifts will most likely come from. By the way, senior executives (like you) can be a part of the shift, but only if they are willing to embrace a new perspective—not just improving on the old ways of doing business, but rather creating new ways.

How to Develop New Paradigms

Now that you've made the commitment to creating new paradigms, where do you begin? If you are the chief executive, you had better look in the mirror and answer the following questions:

What type of environment are you fostering within your business? Are your employees encouraged to explore new avenues, to make mistakes and learn from them? To strike out with bold new ideas? Or is innovative thinking discouraged, shunned, or forbidden? Are you perceived by your employees as a dictator or as an innovative leader, frequently offering encouragement for new ideas?

Once your key employees are empowered by you to discover new paradigms, where do they begin the search? How do you go about generating new paradigms?

There is no one way or right way to develop new paradigms. Ideas can come from virtually anywhere. Fodder for many of my paradigm shifts has come from publications like *Discover* and TV series like *Nova*, both of which frequently discuss cutting-edge ideas. When I travel on business, I constantly engage in discussions with other executives from a variety of industries, asking them probing questions that might reveal innovative new paths their companies are taking.

In my own business, I frequently form "tiger teams" to address critical problems. In forming these teams, if we're looking for a more powerful paradigm in one department (say, engineering), I create a team comprised of a cross-section of disciplines (engineering, marketing, manufacturing, administration), and I always include at least one innovator on each team.

Throw out challenges to your employees. For example, if you have a marketing business, challenge your staff to look at expansions into untapped markets. If you don't find these markets, someone else will. Look what happened to IBM when Apple stepped in.

Provide an environment within your company that encourages frequent discussion of new ideas, through scheduled or impromptu bull sessions where everyone present can express ideas without censorship. In these sessions, focus on such topics as: How can we run the company better? How can we improve production efficiency? Improve customer service? Develop new products for new markets? There are several books on the market that describe brainstorming techniques you can use to stimulate creative ideas.

Never be too quick to condemn an idea as impractical. And never discard an idea just because it has been looked at before. If approached from a different angle, it just might yield a paradigm shift. If you maintain that you have looked at the idea before and were able to advance only so far before being stumped, then put together a "tiger team" to analyze what it was that had you stumped. Consider looking at new technology advances, ideas from other industries, or even low-tech approaches to solve the problems.

As you hire or promote new people into the management ranks, inform them that there are some business practices within their department that are inefficient and costly. Tell them that you recognize these practices, but you want to see how proficient they are at identifying them and recommending changes. If you ensure that these fledglings are not constrained by other staff, you may be amazed at the observations and solutions they come up with.

EXERCISE: Creating the Environment for Transformation

1. Take an inventory in your notebook of the ways you presently conduct business. Focus on those products, services, or activities you most strongly perceive as "perfect" or as "the right way" of doing things. Make sure you cover all aspects of your business, including your management style, your products, how you market your products, how you treat your employees, what level of service you give your customers, and how you view your suppliers and competitors.

This list should give you a good picture of the paradigms that are most firmly entrenched. Now review this list, and ask yourself what problems still exist within each of the key areas of the business. These are potential arenas from which paradigm shifts will emerge.

Next, think about what conditions or events might cause you to alter these "right ways" of doing things. For example, if you currently offer service from nine to five and a major competitor sets up a twenty-four-hour service hotline, how will you respond? List potential actions or conditions that would force you to change the way you do business. This list will help you define potential paradigm shifts you could make—before the competition does it for you.

2. List business practices that other people (competitors, consumers, suppliers, and financiers) engage in that you consider unique, odd, even weird. These hold the potential for paradigm shifts.

Remember the St. Petersburg car dealer? Remember Ted Turner and CNN? Maybe there's a company in your industry that is doing things differently. And maybe the rest of the industry is laughing. But don't you laugh. Instead, think about how the idea of that "oddball" company can be adapted, modified, or expanded so that it gives your company a competitive edge.

3. Next, list specific steps you could take within your business to foster a spirit of change, the willingness to investigate potential paradigm shifts, and the courage to present potential ideas to the executive team. Share the other items in this exercise with your key employees.

4. Finally, I want you to ask yourself: *What things are impossible in my company or industry today that, if they could be done, would fundamentally change my business?*[2] These "impossible dreams" represent areas of the greatest potential for paradigm shifts.

This last question is so important that I want you to consider painting it on a sign and posting it in the boardroom and the employee break area. The key to successful and continuous paradigm shifts within your business is to ask that question again and again, at all levels of the company.

2. Adapted from *Future Edge: Discovering the New Paradigms for Success*, "The Paradigm Shift Question," page 147.

The exercise on page 35 will give you some additional suggestions for stimulating the development of new paradigms. But more important than any exercise is to create the right environment for paradigm shifts. Above all, remember that paradigm shifts won't happen within your company unless the chief executive fosters an environment for change. And that means more than just a memo or a one-time speech. It means constant encouragement and support.

An Ongoing Process

Suppose that six months from now your company perceives and embraces a paradigm shift. You see exciting new markets—and profits—ahead. The temptation will be great to focus all your energies on the new paradigm. Don't do it.

The ongoing analysis of paradigms is an essential element of your company's quest for success. After making a shift to a new paradigm, you must be careful not to embrace it as the absolute, perfect answer. (Remember, that's what gets companies in trouble in the first place.)

As you implement your new paradigm, it will inevitably generate new problems. It is these unsolved problems that can serve as the launching platform for future paradigm shifts—and remember, if you don't explore the possibility of additional shifts, your competition will.

*   *   *

Most companies focus a fair amount of attention on managing the physical and financial assets of the business. But when it comes to the most valuable asset of all—employees—they often fall short. As a result, even if they seem to be doing well, these companies are missing out on valuable opportunities for growth and greater success. In Step Three, you'll learn how to harness the creative power and win the loyalty of workers—the single most important ingredient of sustained success.

Step Three
Build a Dedicated Employee Team

When I started my first company more than two decades ago, my banker and business associate of many years offered me a profound piece of advice. He implored me always to treat my employees as partners, to recognize *them*—not my cash or my other assets—as the primary source of growth and success for my business. He insisted this was the least expensive way to ensure a strong bottom line. His advice has proven its worth many times over in my various businesses.

Think of your company as a team and your employees as team members. If your team is to be as successful as possible, you must have the commitment and the wholehearted effort of all team members. Winning the commitment of your employee team is the focus of Step Three of the Macrofruition process.

The message of this chapter is simple: If you treat your employees as subservient beings, they will respond begrudgingly, with mediocre results. If you treat them with indifference, they will accomplish the minimum required to do their jobs. But if you treat them with dignity and respect, you can elicit their loyalty and their best efforts.

What Motivates Employees

Many senior executives fail to win the commitment of employees because they don't have a good understanding of what motivates their work force. Enterpreneurial CEOs are driven to ensure the success of their businesses. They spend long hours to get the company on solid footing. They

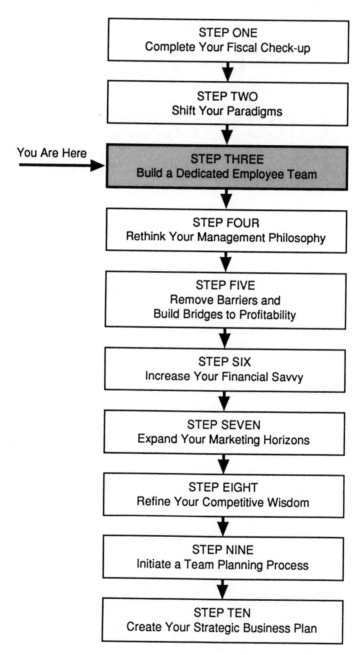

see other team members making the same commitment to long hours and assume they are driven by the same enterpreneurial spirit.

These CEOs tend to be afflicted with what I call Matterhorn Motivation. Armed with super-premium motivation, and, if they are novices, with some degree of business naiveté, these executives are typically overconfident. If you were to hand them a book on mountain climbing equipment, they would eagerly consume it and then consider themselves fully capable of leading an expedition up the Matterhorn.

In contrast, most employees have very different motives. Relatively few employees are enterpreneurs at heart. While you are striving to achieve success for your company, most of your employees want only to achieve a certain level of responsibility, salary, and comfort. They will work hard to get there, but, once they reach that level, they (unlike you) will be satisfied. They will be motivated only to maintain what they have earned with their earlier sacrifices.

Once your employees have reached their goals, they will start practicing risk avoidance, focusing on protecting their positions rather than doing what it takes to make the business continue to succeed. They will carefully filter any information that is a bad reflection on them or their department. As a result, you, as the chief executive, no longer will get a true picture of what is happening in your business.

To avoid or minimize this filtering effect, it's important to keep the lines of communication open to all your employees, not just your direct reports. If you listen only to what your senior executives tell you, you are receiving filtered truth, as opposed to total truth.

Unfortunately, as companies grow, communications tend to deteriorate in direct proportion to the increase in size. Senior executives become immersed in the serious problems that accompany business expansion and become further and further removed from employees. Their attitude toward employees becomes, "Let them take care of themselves. After all, they have managed well in the past."

The problem is that no company lives in the past. Employees are continually subjected to new pressures and stresses for which they are unprepared. Furthermore, in the past, the chief executive was close to employees, right there on the front lines with them, as a source of inspiration and guidance. Now the only communication most employees have with senior management is in the form of memos on company bulletin boards. Whether deliberate or inadvertent, the unspoken message is that senior managers are involved with "more important things" than attending to their employees' needs and concerns.

The High Cost of Mistreating Employees

The kind of benign neglect of employees that I have described is harmful enough. Even worse is the tendency of harried chief executives to take out their frustrations on employees.

Executives are constantly bombarded by company crises. If it isn't a major customer's refusal to pay a sizable debt, it's a banker's refusal to advance additional capital or maybe a supplier's inability to provide needed material on time. Or it's something else—and there is *always* something else.

Many of these encounters are emotionally draining. As an executive, you may be left with scars and raw emotions from dealing with these inevitable confrontations that are part of running a business. Yet you must not allow the leftover emotions from these stressful encounters to influence the manner in which you treat your employees.

Unfortunately, that's what Jane did. Several years ago, Jane, who excelled at her service profession, took the plunge and started her own business in the same industry. Because she had a history of top-quality service to her clients, most of them followed Jane to her new company, and the business grew by leaps and bounds.

Her company's explosive growth occurred during a particularly volatile period in the industry. This created many unforeseen outside pressures for Jane.

Jane had a private office, and her staff of twenty professionals was ensconced in one large room. Periodically, under the pressure of outside business stresses, Jane would blow a fuse and storm out of her office, whereupon she would usually berate one of her staff members in front of the others.

As a result of her habit of venting her frustrations on her employees, Jane has lost their respect; they joke openly about her and her outbursts. But to this day, Jane does not perceive that she has done anything wrong, and she continues to maintain that the employees were reprimanded only when they deserved it.

Jane is now experiencing the consequences of her actions: continuous employee turnover, with the requisite new employee training; a tense "pressure cooker" office environment that is hardly conducive to high productivity; and a staff that will commit to getting the job done, but not much else.

Too bad, because Jane has many creative people on her staff—people who could work with a fervent dedication, without an additional dime in salary, but who instead deliver only a grudging effort. As a result, the company's days of real growth are over.

It doesn't matter if you have twenty employees or twenty thousand. If you treat them as mere tools, or as means to an end, as Jane does, the result will be the same: increased operating costs and diminished bottom line profits. If you protest that you don't need to improve your treatment of employees because *your* profits are steadily rising, I assure you that you are missing out on additional profits that you could achieve, at no extra cost, with a dedicated, committed employee base.

Actions Speak Louder Than Words

Jane's mistreatment of her employees is overt. In many cases, however, maltreatment is more subtle. It shows up in the actions of senior management that show disregard or outright contempt for the feelings of employees.

The double standard is the most common manifestation of this form of abuse. For example, the CEO may preach to employees about the importance of cutting costs but convey a different message by his or her actions. And when two messages are different, employees will always believe the shriek of management action over the mumble of management statements.

Here are two real-life examples of shrieking management actions:

- The chief executive of a $10-million company urges her staff to make sacrifices to cut expenses significantly so the company can continue to show a profit. Then she arrives at work driving an expensive new car bought at company expense. It may seem trivial to her, but it is a slap in the face to the rest of the team.

- The chief executive of another multimillion-dollar company urges his salespeople to make significant sacrifices in order to increase sales in the midst of a recession, "or else." Then the executive is featured in the local newspaper in an article describing his new multimillion-dollar home.

These executives, by their actions, are demonstrating that they care more for their own "piece of the action" than they do for their employees. And rest assured, their employees know it and will respond accordingly, by reducing their effort on the job.

If chief executives are dedicated to their employees, the employees know it and will move mountains to ensure the company's success. But if the executives are dedicated only to themselves, their businesses will gradually decay from within, and ill-treated employees will probably spread the word about the company's impending demise.

Turnover: The Barometer of Employee Satisfaction

The quickest way to determine how well you are treating your employees is to examine your turnover rate. Several years ago, Bill, the owner of a growing business, complained to me that he never seemed to have time to get ahead because he was constantly training new personnel. I asked him what his salaried employee turnover rate was; he said it had been more than 10 percent the previous year. I told him this barometer reading implied that a turbulent storm was brewing, one that could develop into a major disaster unless he corrected the underlying problem.

I explained to Bill that, according to my company's past management surveys (for a growing business with satisfactory wages and benefits) an annual attrition rate of less than 5 percent among salaried employees indicates that employees are generally satisfied. A rate between 5 and 10 percent can be a sign of emerging problems. An attrition rate much above 10 percent suggests deep-seated morale problems, with employees too fearful to discuss their problems with management.

I suggested that Bill allow our firm to conduct an employee feedback survey to assess the reason for the high turnover rate. Bill accepted my suggestion, and our survey results were quite startling. Although I saw my business associate as an astute, honest, and skilled businessman, his employees saw him as an ogre who humiliated them in front of other employees.

When I confronted Bill with the results of the survey, he was shocked. He believed that a good manager must act like a drill sergeant in order to gain the respect of his people and avoid having them take advantage of him. I pointed out that this strategy might work in war, but it was disastrous in business.

During further discussions, Bill confided in me that his attitude may have been a holdover from the way he was treated as a child. I asked if he believed he could change; he said he could not. I told him that in my opinion he would either lose his health or his business within the next few years if he didn't bring in a more compassionate general manager to run the company.

Three months later, to his credit, Bill turned the company reins over to a manager experienced in employee motivation. Within the following year, the company's salaried employee turnover rate was cut in half.

The cost of turnover, in terms of lost productivity and time, and money and effort spent in hiring and training new workers, can be enormous. When turnover is abnormally high, unless the company is offering substandard wages, the reason is usually found in the executive suite. If you are experiencing an excessive employee turnover problem and can't find the cause, you might try looking in the closest mirror.

How to Keep Employees Satisfied

Thus far we have discussed a number of symptoms and causes of employee dissatisfaction. Left unattended, this dissatisfaction is sure to undermine the productivity of your company. Now it's time to focus on methods of corrective action, many of which are surprisingly straightforward.

The Ten *P*s of Employee Satisfaction

To help executive managers promote employee satisfaction within their businesses, several years ago I developed the ten *P*s of Employee Satisfaction (see Figure 3-1). If you jot down these ten *P* words on a small card and put the card where you will notice it frequently, you will find yourself more readily able to promote activities that enhance employee commitment. The ten *P*s are:

1. *Pay.* Reward your people with a wage commensurate with their efforts. If you choose to provide employees with a meager wage, they will respond with a meager effort. But if you give them a generous paycheck, they will respond with generous performance. As the old saying goes, you get what you pay for.

If you have key executives you don't want to lose, make sure you pay them what they're worth. If this means a cash flow problem in tough times, structure their compensation so they receive a smaller base salary with a significant performance bonus that is tied to the company's strategic plan.

Then define specific goals and responsibilities for each key manager—activities that will contribute to the success of the strategic plan. If there are critical near-term goals for the company, factor this into the compensation package by creating specific additional one-time year-end bonuses for select executives if they accomplish critical strategic objectives.

Most companies set up bonus systems only for their executives. But there's no reason why you can't structure performance-based compensation packages for all your employees, including hourly workers. Just make sure that you tie their bonuses to performance measures over which they have some control. By offering the opportunity for all employees to earn bonuses, you send a powerful positive message that you're all in this together.

2. *Praise.* Praising individual employees is one of the most effective ways to increase company morale and productivity without investing additional dollars. We all like to be told when we've done a good job. Praise makes us work just that much harder. It improves the morale of all employees, not just the praised individual.

Let your employees know (both individually and collectively) when they have done a job well. Actively seek out opportunities to compliment your employees. Kenneth Blanchard said it best when he encouraged managers to catch their employees "doing something right."

Praising should usually be done publicly, before the appropriate staff members, and also in private, one to one, letting the outstanding individuals know that their actions have benefited the company and that you truly appreciate their efforts.

Conduct your private praising first. Then, follow up with the public praising as soon as possible.

3. *Probe.* Many years ago I coined the term "diode management." A diode is an electrical component that allows current to flow in one direction but not the other. A company with diode management has an environment in which information (usually directives) flows in one direction only—from the top down. You can be sure that such a company is not realizing the full potential of its employees.

If you truly believe your employees are an important asset, then ask for their input. Let them know that their opinions and suggestions are vital to the ongoing success of the company.

There are many ways to ensure that you spend time listening to your employees, not just giving them directives. One of my favorites is the monthly lunch. Once a month, consider inviting four or five employees to join you for lunch, at company expense. Select an upscale restaurant with a quiet atmosphere so you can talk easily. Then discuss some of your plans, ideas, and concerns with the group members, and invite them to discuss theirs with you (and try to do more listening than talking).

Each month, choose different employees representing a cross-section of the company (in terms of departments and status). The group should not include your direct reports, and, ideally, no more than one person from a given department should be invited. The employees will view the lunch as a desirable perquisite, and you will find it a valuable source of information.

Another way to make sure you're getting employee input is to have suggestion boxes. But beware: If you don't accompany this with a review committee, it may do more harm than good. Nothing is worse for an employee's morale than to offer suggestions, only to have them ignored. The suggestion review committee should comprise executives, managers, and hourly personnel, and it should make appropriate recommendations to the company president.

Offer the originator of an accepted suggestion some sign of recognition, say, a jacket or a plaque. Or you might consider following NASA's lead and offer the author a piece of the action (in the early stages of the space program, NASA offered a small "commission" on the overall monetary savings achieved during a specified term as a result of a winning suggestion).

4. *Proclaim.* Whether good news or bad, report company results, plans, and significant events to your employees. A written newsletter is a start in the right direction, but a frequent "fireside chat" with all employees is far better. At least once a quarter I try to conduct a companywide briefing. Each of these briefings may have a different purpose: to describe a new product unveiling before the public announcement, to go over the company's results during the previous period, or to discuss a reorganization of the company.

Offer details about your products to employees. I started holding regular product briefings in my first company, an electronics manufacturing concern, after a production-line worker asked me how the circuit board she was assembling was utilized in the end product. After I answered her, it dawned on me that the production crew knew little about our finished products and that maybe they were interested in knowing more.

Thereafter, once a month I opened my boardroom to a specific production team. They brought in their lunch boxes, and I brought in one of our trade show demonstrators. While the employees ate, I gave them a detailed product presentation. They asked many probing questions, some of which led to product improvements.

Even though it meant sacrificing their lunch hour, the employees always packed the boardroom for these "show and tell" presentations and clamored for more, because the demonstrations helped them to understand how their individual efforts contributed to the bigger picture.

5. *Participate.* Join in company activities, and always be accessible to your employees. Being aloof gives you the image of an uncaring taskmaster and serves to magnify other problems.

Institute an open-door policy, whereby every executive is available during a specific thirty-minute period each week (try Monday morning if most managers won't be traveling at that time). The objective here is to encourage employees to visit, not only with their supervisors, but with anyone they care to (including you). The meetings should be no more than five to ten minutes in length, so you can accommodate several meetings each week.

Although these meetings may bring forth some trivial concerns, they will also afford you the opportunity to uncover critical festering issues that would have otherwise gone unnoticed until they had erupted into serious problems.

Company parties are another good way of maintaining camaraderie with employees. But they are beneficial only if all the top executives attend.

6. *Promote.* Through your review and goal-setting process, provide visible paths for advancement within the organization. Let employees see that hard work and dedication pay off with promotions.

Prior to each of my employee's reviews, I analyze the person's managerial strengths and weaknesses, along with the most probable career path within the company. Then I envision what goals the worker could establish to improve his or her management potential.

During the review process, the employee and I agree to specific goals that the employee should strive to achieve, some within six months and others within twelve months. I try to guide each employee I review, so that the goals I envision for that employee are incorporated into his or her individual objectives. These goals might include improving work flow, organizing a committee, developing a production plan, preparing a company workshop, or taking a continuing education course on effective employee interaction.

Through this review process, I guide employee growth for the benefit of the company. Employees, on the other hand, perceive (rightly) that I'm actively interested in their personal as well as their professional development. Using this technique, I am also able to groom key employees for future leadership positions.

7. *Proffer.* Offer continuing education programs and opportunities for your employees to improve themselves. They will look on such

opportunities as another benefit, but you will reap the benefits of improved productivity.

Some of these programs and classes may be offered through university extension programs; others may be offered as national workshops in your city or by area training organizations. When you learn of an upcoming workshop covering a topic you want to promote to your employees, distribute a memo to key staff members if you want to limit attendance. If you want to encourage department (or companywide) attendance, post a notice and a sign-up sheet on departmental or company bulletin boards. In any event, contact those specific employees you would like to have attend and encourage them to sign up.

Don't be too quick to veto some choices your employees may come up with on their own. In my first company, several of my production line supervisors wanted to take a course in "assertive management." I thought they were assertive enough, but in the end, I supported their request. As part of this course, they learned how to negotiate with their subordinates and became much more effective at handling employee complaints in a constructive manner. The moral: Employees often know best what training they need.

8. *Provide.* Employees need symbols or emblems of the company that they can display with pride. These might be hats, jackets, coffee cups, or wall plaques. Let them share their enthusiasm for your company with others, and the word will get around that you have a successful business.

These symbols don't have to be taken seriously in order to have a serious impact. During a difficult period for my first company, as a joke I ordered a few T-shirts colored a hideous purple and emblazoned with our company's logo. That week I presented one to our "employee of the month." She began to wear the dreadful thing, and it became a status symbol. Soon other employees were asking how they could win one.

So we developed a series of contests involving productivity goals, with the winners receiving their very own purple shirts. The sense of dedication and camaraderie that had been missing returned, and company productivity increased.

9. *Perfect.* No company is organized perfectly the first time around. As your business continues to grow and expand, always be open to revising your operating system and organizational structure to maximize productivity. (But beware of changing just for the sake of change. If it ain't broke, don't fix it.)

My first company's initial product line was a series of electronic monitoring systems for agriculture. We created a national organization of agricultural sales representatives to market our products nationwide. These reps called on the dealers who serviced farmers. They were efficient at getting dealers to place initial orders, but we saw little repeat business because our reps were used to dealing with low-tech products and didn't understand how to sell our system.

After some serious soul-searching, we scuttled the organization of agricultural sales representatives and created a new organization using electronics sales reps. These reps were far more successful because they focused on the distributors who sold products to farm dealers and helped train the dealer organizations.

10. *Perform.* Nothing succeeds like success. By creating and sustaining a dynamic, prosperous business, you will give your employees a company they can take pride in. Your employees are a vital asset in helping the company achieve success, but they still need a leader at the helm. It's up to you to perform at your personal best in order to ensure growth and prosperity and to inspire confidence and commitment in your employees.

Note that my ten *P* words are all verbs; they require some action on your part. If you make a concerted effort to give your employees the message that they are your most important asset, you should begin to realize an increased level of performance from your staff.

Make Your Business a Game

My first company started small and grew steadily. In the early years, everybody pitched in, doing whatever needed to be done, from packing a major order to testing a new product concept to building a new trade show demonstrator. My employees came up with more ideas than I did about how to run the business. We had a lot of fun, naturally—the thrill of seeing the business come to life. We worked hard, but we all had a great time.

As the company grew beyond fifty employees, we lost the sense of closeness and the enjoyment that went with it. I was no longer seen as a teammate by the new hires. I noticed that my employees no longer seemed to feel a sense of excitement, as we all had in the early days. I remember remarking to one of my original employees that the sparkle had gone out of her eyes. She responded that her job wasn't as much fun as it used to be, because in the early days she was creating something, whereas now she was just doing a job.

Figure 3-1. The ten Ps of employee satisfaction.

1. PAY	Reward your employees with a wage commensurate with their efforts.
2. PRAISE	Let your employees know (individually and collectively) when they have done a job well.
3. PROBE	If you believe your emloyees are an important asset, ask for their input.
4. PROCLAIM	Whether good news or bad, report company results, plans, and significant events to your employees.
5. PARTICIPATE	Join in company activities, and always be accessible to your employees.
6. PROMOTE	Through your review and goal-setting process, provide visible paths for advancement within the organization.
7. PROFFER	Offer continuing education programs and opportunities for your employees to improve themselves.
8. PROVIDE	Offer symbols or emblems of the company that employees can display with pride. Let them share their enthusiasm for your company with others, and the word will get around that you have a successful business.
9. PERFECT	No company is organized perfectly the first time around. As your business continues to grow and expand, always be open to revising your operating system and organizational structure to maximize productivity.
10. PERFORM	Nothing succeeds like success. It's up to you to perform at your personal best in order to ensure growth and prosperity and to inspire confidence and commitment in your employees.

Ouch. That comment made me realize that in most businesses, employees believe they are just doing a job. And my business was becoming just like all the rest.

Remember what I said earlier about the difference in motivation between founders and employees? Let me add a point here: While your goal is to maximize productivity and profits, your employees' goal is to have an exciting and rewarding work environment. And if you hope to keep your employees enthusiastic about the business, you had better provide one.

After my employee's painful comment, I latched onto the idea of creating what I call "The Game." In fact, it was a series of games designed to get employees involved in the details of the business and to recapture the spirit of fun and enjoyment that came so naturally in the early days of the company.

I started small. The first game involved creating employee committees to oversee the monies that were collected in the company vending machines. Employees who were accustomed to responding to directives from above were now told to take the proceeds of the machines (about $500 a year) and decide how to use them. We had some terrific parties as a result, including one where we roasted a pig.

The next game involved setting productivity and profit goals for each department. Every game has rules. In order to play this and subsequent games, my employees had to learn the rules of the business—what made our company profitable, what made us "lose a turn" and get behind the competition. To play the game well, they had to understand such things as the difference between equity and debt, gross and net profits, why business expenses and taxes were higher than those they faced, and what they could do to control them.

To educate employees about these "rules" and to further the game spirit, we began to hold classes after work in which I'd explain some details about how the company was run and how financial statements were read. These classes were optional; there was no pressure for anybody to show up. But more and more employees began to attend. I found they were eager to learn and understand the business to the best of their individual abilities, and they all wanted the company to succeed.

Next, we launched one training course in reading financial statements, one in computers, and another in our products. We also began posting a monthly summary of the company's financial statements, as well as a status report on each department's progress toward its goals. When a particularly noteworthy goal was achieved, such as a major new order or large shipment, we held a company kegger on Friday night to celebrate.

By now, the business felt like a game. Employees were experiencing the excitement of winning. And while they were having fun with the games we devised, productivity was increasing.

Whenever new challenges arose (which is frequently in a growing business), our executive team met with the departments involved to plot together the best course of action. The employees' ideas and energy were amazing. When times were tough, I would brief all employees as much as I could, so they didn't feel in the dark. In response, they gave their commitment and loyalty.

I can't overemphasize what a difference these games made in the morale and productivity of my employees. Over the years, the games elicited many creative ideas that saved the company money. We always shared the savings with the employee whose idea was implemented.

Long after I launched my own games, I discovered I wasn't the only one who had experimented with ways to make the business more enjoyable and challenging for employees. I read about Jack Stack, a middle manager with International Harvester Corporation, who was assigned to an IH subsidiary, Springfield Manufacturing Company (SMC), to turn the company around. At the time, SMC, a rebuilder of engines and engine components, was losing $2 million a year on revenues of $26 million.

Stack arrived at SRC in Springfield, Missouri, to find the company awash in red ink, workers demoralized, and a critical parts shortage that had almost ground production to a halt. So he created what he called the "Great Game of Business," in which all employees participated. The game involved setting detailed productivity goals for all departments. Stack began by focusing on several areas, which he called "accountabilities"—product quality, safety, housekeeping (the cleanliness and orderliness of each work area)—and set specific production goals.

The employees loved the challenge. Within nine months, the losing subsidiary was transformed into a profitable business. Stack and his team went on to buy the company, which has current revenues in excess of $50 million, with all employees owning a piece of the action.

Rick Stewart, founder of Frontier Herbs in Norway, Iowa, created his own version of the game. What started in 1976 as a free service to repackage herbs and spices into smaller packages has grown into a multimillion-dollar business, but Stewart had to learn the business of running a business along the way.

Stewart started with his belief that people will do what needs to be done only if they are having fun. As his enterprise grew beyond a home-based family operation, he kept the fun in the business for all his employees. His company provides employees with a full day-care facility on site, and employees are free to visit their children at any time during the day. He also provides an on-site health club facility and a full hot lunch every day, all at no cost to the employees.

Stewart believes in a bonus plan, as opposed to profit sharing (with a bonus plan the employee is rewarded on the basis of individual performance, rather than overall company profitability). Each employee writes his or her own annual bonus goals. Stewart's program continues to be effective—current sales stand at $15 million, with continued growth of 30 percent each year—and in 1992 Stewart was selected as runner-up for the Small Business Administration's National Small Business Person of the Year.

EXERCISE: Unleashing Employee Potential

Now that you've studied Step Three, take time for some soul-searching. Even if you are happy with your company's current results, there are actions you can take to improve the bottom line with no increase in expenses.

Create a new section in your notebook called "Unleashing Employee Potential." Start your contemplative process by reviewing the Ten *P*s from Figure 3-1. How do you measure up to each? Where could you do better?

Now that you've warmed up, write several paragraphs about those actions you can take to make your employees perceive themselves as participants in the company's success, as opposed to mere spectators.

Now sit back and look at what you have written. Can these individual initiatives be forged into a cohesive program to encourage and utilize continuing support from your employees?

Everybody likes a challenge. People enjoy the thrill of a game. If you can turn your business into a game, if your employees view their jobs as an exciting challenge, as something that is fun rather than work, you won't have to worry about productivity problems.

Turning your business into a game is not without its problems. As employees become more involved and take on more responsibility for winning the game, they're bound to make mistakes, but this is all part of the learning experience. You weren't able to stay up on your bicycle the first time, either, but look at you now. If you help them to try, show them you care, and give them the tools they need, your employees will move mountains for you.

Remember the banker I mentioned at the beginning of this chapter, the one who introduced me to the hidden power within my employees? He has since done very well, progressing from loan officer to CEO of a major financial institution. If you have the courage to follow his advice, you, too, can unleash the dormant power within your staff and achieve that boost in productivity predicted by my banker.

* * *

After my first company merged with an international conglomerate, I went on to create another technology-driven firm. We hit the ground running and achieved a production backlog of almost $10 million our first year.

You would think that my earlier experiences as an employer would have ensured success with my second company. Not so. I almost lost sight of my employees, until I realized that there are two stages in motivating employees. The first is *creating* the right environment, which I have covered in this chapter. The second stage is *sustaining* the process, which is the subject of Step Four, on revising your management philosophy.

Step Four
Rethink Your Management Philosophy

In this chapter, we shift our focus from employees to management. In Step Four you'll learn how to make the transition from *being* a leader to *becoming* a manager. We'll review the pros and cons of various management styles and techniques. We'll outline the managerial actions needed to ensure the continued success of your company, under your leadership and beyond. Finally, we'll focus on the extra steps you can take to put your company on the cutting edge.

Many chief executives, having fought and won the major battles for initial company success, see themselves maturing into wise parents, believing they know what is best for their employee-children. The result is that these executives, often unconsciously, exhibit a demeaning, condescending attitude—hardly the environment to foster the continued growth of a management-employee team.

Consider the dilemma of Marie, president of a successful business of three hundred people, who came to me with a problem. She had recently offered improved health plan benefits to her employees. Marie expected them to be grateful, but they were disappointed because they had anticipated an increase in their wages. Marie wanted to know how to resolve the dilemma.

I took a tablet and drew a silhouette of a human body. I gave the drawing to Marie, telling her it represented the corporate body of her company, and asked her to indicate what portion of the body symbolized her as chief executive. She circled the head, hands, and feet, explaining it was she who made the decisions and took effective action to ensure goals were met.

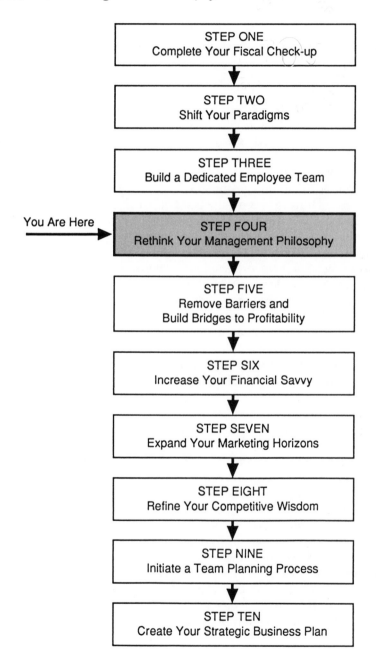

I suggested that her belief that *she* accomplished everything was bound to alienate her employees. I tossed her another drawing of the silhouette and asked her to try again by indicating what she *should* be. This time she circled the head, commenting that she should be the brains of the organization.

I drew a third figure, but this time I circled the upper chest and suggested that *this* was what she should strive to be—the heart, the lifeblood, the driving force, giving to the other parts of the corporate body so they could grow.

That was what she was doing with the medical plan, she protested. I explained it was a useless gesture if her employees really didn't want it.

She asked how to become the heart of her company. I explained that it would be difficult; she would need to change her long-held views on her "presidential" relationship with her employees. She currently saw her employees as working *for* her. She needed to see them as working *with* her. Although she was expected to provide leadership, her primary responsibility was not to "boss" her employees, but to provide them with the resources they needed to get the job done, thus ensuring the corporate body of the business would continue to grow.

I am happy to report that Marie subsequently solved her problem by asking for input from her employees. The result was a scaled-back health plan (with additional employee-paid options), coupled with a small wage increase, paid out of the health plan savings.

From Leader to Manager

When my first child was born I stood in awe, looking at the small, helpless being I had helped create, knowing this child needed my constant attention to survive. Now, decades later, I often find my grown children showing *me* the way, teaching me new things.

So it is with your business. As your company grows, it takes on a life of its own. And just as parents find it necessary to alter their relationship with their children as they emerge into adulthood, so must you alter your association with your employees. In the early days of any company, it is vital that the founder lead the way. But at some point, it's necessary to make the transition from being a leader to becoming a manager, thereby becoming the "heart" of your organization.

Unfortunately, entrepreneurial executives tend to be good leaders but lousy managers. They may be great at assembling the troops, inspiring them, and leading the charge, but, as the company grows, they often do a poor job of passing their authority to others, which is the central task of management. Because the chief executive has spent so long controlling the entire company during its early growth period, it is difficult for him or her to relinquish any portion of that absolute control to other team members.

I know this from painful experience. After I wore all the hats in my first company for five years, I finally had to hire a marketing manager. It was agonizing to pass on the responsibility for a key new product to him. I was sure I could manage the marketing effort better myself, and I couldn't afford a failure.

My new marketing manager proceeded to sign up a popular TV actor as our national spokesman for the new product. The actor worked on a pure commission basis, which cost us no money up front, and landed us on the cover of several magazines. The free publicity paid off in spades. Product sales took off like a rocket, and I had to face reality: My new marketing manager had done a more effective job than I would have.

To make a successful transition to becoming a true manager, you must learn to relinquish control. You must give the rest of your team members the authority and the freedom to produce results. This is the only way your company can hope to achieve its maximum potential.

This doesn't mean that you have to give up *all* control over your company; it just means that you must share your power. It is popular nowadays to talk about inverting the corporate pyramid, with you working for your employees. I believe an even better approach is to turn the pyramid *on its side,* with productive efforts flowing in both directions and everybody working in partnership for the betterment of the business. If you can make this change in perspective, if you become comfortable with delegating some of your power and authority to the rest of your management team, you can amplify productivity without paying a single additional penny in wages.

Although insecure chief executives may see this perspective as a threat, strong executives see it as a virtue. So do bankers. Your financiers perceive greater risk if you stay in the leadership rut and avoid the transition to management. The reason is simple. Your financial backers want assurances that, if they lend you $500,000 today and you get hit by a truck tomorrow, the business will continue to operate profitably. If a bank examines your company and sees that it doesn't have sufficient management depth to cover contingencies, you won't see any of its money.

Making the transition from leader to manager is never easy, precisely because it involves sharing power (turning the pyramid on its side). But as your business grows, there will come a point where you simply can no longer cover all the bases yourself. At that point you must become an effective manager or your company will atrophy into insignificance.

Consider the case of Jeff and Pete. Both started similar retail businesses, and both subsequently expanded with additional outlets. After five years, both companies enjoyed approximately equal sales and profits. However, Jeff continued to rule his company with an iron hand, making all major decisions himself, while Pete successfully advanced into a management role, passing much of his authority to his managers.

Four years later, Pete's company was still expanding, whereas Jeff's sales continued to drop, and many of his outlets closed. Jeff's foolish pride cost him the realization of his dream.

If you haven't already done so, begin to let go and share responsibility with your employees, despite the little voice inside your head that whispers that you could do it better. Dare to let your subordinates tackle tough tasks that require more experience. Then critique their accomplishments.

The result? Your staff will accomplish more for the business when they act as an experienced management team, and your company will be on its way to a more productive future. And if you should become disabled, your battle-hardened employees will keep the company on course.

What If I Don't Want to Manage?

So far I've talked about how vital it is to make the transition from leadership to management. But what if you don't want to manage?

If you don't want to take on the role of manager, you're not alone. If you are like most senior executives of growing companies, you have found that more and more of your time is spent in administrative activities, and you may be finding that running the company just isn't as much fun as it used to be. If you are an executive with genuine entrepreneurial drive, the increasing administrative activities can put you in a real funk.

You must ask yourself if you are content to manage, or whether you'd rather stay in a creative role. If your answer is the latter, bring in someone else to run the company while you remain as senior vice-president of research and development or take on whatever other position you prefer. It's important to you, and to the rest of the company, that you make the decision that will ensure that you continue having fun with the business. If you perceive your job as drudgery, imagine the message you will send to the rest of your team.

Management Techniques

Management techniques involve specific ways of dealing with employees. Managers may use different techniques with different employees; for example, you would probably deal with a belligerent employee differently than a dedicated one.

In *Leadership and the One Minute Manager*[1] (a book I heartily recommend for all managers), the authors identify two basic types of managerial behavior: *directive behavior*, which involves such activities as controlling, supervising, and structuring, and *supportive behavior*, which involves key activities, such as praising, listening, and facilitating, that support the work of others. These behaviors are associated with four fundamental management techniques.[2] The best technique to use varies with different employees and different situations. Unless you have employees with equal experience, ability, and drive, you should not use the same management technique with all of them.

The *directing* technique involves providing specific instructions and close supervision. It requires the manager to exercise high directive behavior and low supportive behavior. The directing technique is appropriate for inexperienced people and for employees who may have some experience but are new to the company and don't yet know your goals and way of doing business. It is also appropriate when a decision has to be made quickly and the stakes are high.

The *coaching* technique requires the manager to exercise both high directive behavior and high supportive behavior. It involves direction and supervision, but it also includes explaining decisions, soliciting suggestions, and supporting employee progress. When the initial excitement of being a new employee wears off or when an experienced employee gives evidence of a drop in commitment or makes slow progress, coaching is the best management technique to use.

Next is the *supporting* technique, which requires the manager to exercise low directive behavior coupled with high supportive behavior. This technique involves facilitating and supporting subordinates' efforts and sharing decision making with them. When your subordinates have

1. Ken Blanchard, Patricia Zigarmi, and Drea Zigarmi, *Leadership and the One Minute Manager* (New York: Morrow, 1985).
2. *Leadership and the One Minute Manager* comes from the perspective of teaching all company managers to be leaders, whereas my books focus on the perspective of teaching chief executives who are already leaders to become managers. Therefore, although Blanchard et al. refer to the *four basic leadership styles*, within our context these are referred to as the *four fundamental management techniques*.

more experience and no longer need direction but still lack the ability to manage tasks totally on their own, this is the best management technique to use.

Finally, there is the *delegating* technique. Like the supporting technique, it involves facilitating and supporting subordinates' efforts and sharing decision making with them. But delegating requires the manager to exercise both low supportive behavior and low directive behavior. This technique requires turning over responsibility and accountability for decision making and problem solving to the subordinate. Use this management technique with your peak performers, the true self-starters who are experienced, competent, and committed.

Not surprisingly, employees tend to progress from needing direction to needing coaching to needing support to needing delegation. Your goal is to get all your subordinates at a level where you use the delegating technique with all of them so you can devote more time to running the business. But be careful: If you attempt the transition from one technique to the next too soon, you'll end up spending a lot of time and money correcting employees' mistakes, and you may lose some good people along the way.

EXERCISE: Your Appropriate Management Techniques

Open your notebook and prepare a list of six or more of your key first reports. Opposite each person's name, write down which one of the four management techniques just discussed is most appropriate in dealing with that individual at this time. Remember, your goal is to move everyone toward the delegating technique. For each person on your list, what specific actions can you take during the next quarter to move him or her closer to readiness for this technique?

CARE: The Formula for Sustained Success

Now you have a basic knowledge of the management styles and techniques available and how to relate to your employees. But there's more work ahead. Unless you continue to inspire and motivate your employees, your business will fall short of achieving its true potential.

There are four basic actions you must take to ensure the ongoing success of your business: You must Communicate with employees;

*A*ssess your management style and progress at regular intervals; *R*esearch ways to improve the business; and *E*nhance operations as needed, in response to your findings from the first three steps. In other words, you must *CARE*.

Action 1: Communicate

As I mentioned in Step Three, entrepreneurial executives may have good communications with employees during the company's early years. But as the business grows, matures, and begins to achieve some measure of success, the executive's responsibilities—and life style—change, and inevitably the relationship with employees changes as well. Many executives at this point no longer work at sustaining communications with employees, and productivity suffers as a result.

The most effective executives are "walk-around" managers. They believe in being out on the firing line with their employees, talking with and listening to the troops. No matter how demanding their schedule is, they try to visit some of the rank-and-file workers each day, asking questions and giving words of encouragement. As a result, their employees know they care.

More important, these managers know what is happening within the corridors of their company. If they see the potential for a problem, they can resolve it long before it becomes an issue affecting the bottom line.

Action 2: Assess

Which of these provides a more accurate assessment of the success of your management style—the way *you* perceive you are performing or the way *your subordinates* perceive you are performing? You may wish it were the former, but in fact it is the latter. Your perception of your management style indicates how you *intend* to act. Your employees' perception indicates how you *are* acting.

Business executives often find themselves so enmeshed in the rigors of day-to-day operations that they fail to take the time to assess how well they are performing. As a result, many growing, profitable companies have a festering, deep-seated management problem that is not being addressed. The inevitable result is depressed productivity and profits that are lower than they should be.

I am frequently engaged as a consultant by companies suffering from a phantom productivity problem in one of their plants or divisions. Management knows productivity is low but can't ascertain why. By acting as an intermediary between employees and management (thereby guaranteeing confidentiality to the employees), I uncover dangerous yet predictable environments. Disillusioned, frustrated, and angry employees who believe they are being ignored, taken advantage of, lied to, or victimized by a double standard are far less proficient in their jobs. After this malignancy has thoroughly permeated an organization, management may be powerless to curtail its insidious results. So management pays me a fee to come in and discover what it should have already known.

To prevent these inefficiencies and lost profits, it is imperative that you, as a senior executive, develop a systematic method of measuring your management performance, with a portion of this assessment coming from subordinate employees. This assessment is a three-step process.

First, set your own written goals, to be achieved at six-month intervals. Then, every six months, take out the list of goals, write an assessment of your performance against those goals, and modify them or establish follow-up goals for the next six months. Pay attention to the percentage of goals being accomplished each review period. (We discuss goal-setting in detail later in this chapter, in the section on developing your managerial map.)

Second, periodically offer your first reports and other select employees the opportunity to rate your performance, candidly assessing your strengths and weaknesses. (How to carry out these evaluations is covered in detail in a later section on peer review.)

Third, because certain facets of your management personality may promote productivity within your business while other facets impede it, you should periodically try to identify any personality weaknesses that affect how you deal with employees.[3] Also, periodically review your general management techniques (directing, coaching, supporting, delegating) to determine whether you are using the appropriate technique with individual employees.

The result of these three efforts will reveal the steps you need to take in order to become a more effective manager of people. We discuss these activities in more detail later in this chapter.

Action 3: Research

As the chief executive of a company that has achieved some measure of success, you have two choices: You can either forge ahead and make

---

3. One way to accomplish this is by periodically taking the Management Personality Quiz available from the HTC Group, P.O. Box 592, Marion, Iowa 52302. (Order item #MPQ103A for $5.95 postpaid.)

further changes in the way you do business or you can maintain the status quo. But be advised that the key to success is *never to stand still*.

Executives committed to maximizing the potential of their companies know that the process of learning and changing never ends (after all, that's why you're reading this book). They know that processes, products, people's needs, regulations, markets, and the economy are constantly changing. Through the process of discovery—whether through books, seminars, classes, or discussions—these executives develop the art of anticipating what the future will hold for their business so that they can modify the business accordingly.

How well are you doing in the research department? If you believe your personal inactivity is caused by the demands of your business, you will soon find your business suffering from that same inactivity.

Action 4: Enhance

Once you have assessed your strengths and weaknesses in the areas of communicating, managing, and research, it's time to implement the necessary changes in order to *enhance* your business. I recommend that you prepare a written list of objectives to be accomplished in order to remedy the weaknesses you identified in the earlier Action steps. Go through each Action step, listing objectives for improving your skills and establishing a short-term time frame for accomplishing each objective. Then keep this list, along with the goals you will be developing in the next section, and review it every six months to check on your progress.

Developing Your Managerial Map

When caught up in the pressures of running a dynamic business, most executives overlook the critical first step in their personal planning process: developing a written list of goals. As a result, they lack a sense of direction. Your written goals serve as your road map. The purpose of your goal-setting map, like any road map, is to make your own journey as efficient and successful as possible.

If you have already established your professional goals, that's great. However, if your goals are in mental form only, they don't count. *A goal that isn't written down is only a wish*. Mental goals have a way of modifying themselves over time, so you can't judge your progress accurately. Write down your goals and tuck them away in your safe deposit box, keeping an extra copy in your wallet or desk drawer for easy reference.

Each of your goals should be specific and measurable and should have a time frame attached, with some goals to be accomplished within six months to a year, others to be accomplished within two to three years, and still others to be reached within five years. Try for a list of ten goals, with at least half to be accomplished within the next six months. Ideally, the remainder should be structured so you can measure some progress within each six-month period.

Every six months thereafter, retrieve your written goals, and review them. Write a one-page assessment of your performance (noting where you performed well and indicating those areas that need a concerted effort during the next six months). Attach this assessment to the front of the sheet with the original goals.

Then, take a clean sheet and write a revised set of goals for the next six months, reflecting changes in your business life since the last set was written. Attach your new goals to the front of the growing packet (again, keep a current copy of your goals in your desk so that you can refer to it whenever you are faced with an important decision). Often the best business decisions will support your established goals. In fact, if they don't, you may want to consider adding some goals to your list during your next review.

It's also a good idea, from time to time, to review your past three or four written assessments to determine trends in your performance.

Peer Review

All of your employees are evaluated on an annual basis, so at least once a year you should invite them to evaluate you and the other senior managers of the company. The best way to handle this event is to have each department conduct a peer review. Ask your first reports to rate each other and to rate you, while all your executives ask their subordinates to rate one another and their executive manager, and so forth. Carry this process as far down the chain of command as you are comfortable, but at least to the lowest level of management in your organization.

A sample of a form you can use for this evaluation is presented in Figure 4-1.

You will receive the most honest feedback if this evaluation is administered by someone outside your organization. If this is not feasible, then it should be administered by the chief executive's administrative assistant (so it still has the power of the president's office). It should not

Figure 4-1. Evaluation form for peers and subordinates.

Confidential Management Evaluation

Part I—Instructions

The purpose of this evaluation is to provide you the opportunity to assist in the preparation of an honest appraisal of the management staff of our company. Because of the importance of your feedback, we ask you to be completely candid in your opinions and assessments. The purpose of this evaluation is not to punish or reward anyone. To protect your confidentiality, we are not asking for your name on this form.

Responses will be held in strictest confidence. Managers being evaluated will not read individual evaluations. All individual evaluations will be combined into a composite evaluation, and only this composite will be provided to the managers in order to assist them in developing their personal and professional growth plans.

You may have several appraisal pages in this packet—one for each member of the management team you will be evaluating. Please complete each page by filling in the blanks or circling the number that most closely relates to your assessment regarding that particular issue.

In all questions asking for a number to be circled, 4 is the best possible ranking, 2 is average, and 0 is the poorest ranking. Note: If you honestly feel that you have not worked long enough with a specific person to respond to a particular question, leave it blank; however, please answer all the questions you possibly can.

Because of the confidential nature of this document, please complete it now, fold it, and deposit it in the box provided before you leave the room.

Thanks for your help.

[signed by the chief executive of the company]

Part II—Appraisal Form

Management Team Member being rated on this page: _____

1. What is this person's job title or responsibility? _____
2. What is your opinion of this person's knowledge relative to his/her area of responsibility?
   [0 is worst, and 4 is best] (Circle Number)
   0   1   2   3   4
3. What is your opinion of this person's ability as a manager? (Circle)
   0   1   2   3   4
4. How effective is this person in relating to other employees? (Circle)
   0   1   2   3   4
5. How would you rate this person's integrity? (Circle)
   0   1   2   3   4
6. What do you perceive as this person's strengths?_____
   _____
   _____ (write on back if needed)
7. What do you perceive as this person's weaknesses? _____
   _____
   _____ (write on back if needed)
8. If you were this person's supervisor and you had to give him/her an overall rating in a single sentence, what would you say? _____
   _____
   _____ (write on back if needed)
9. Any other comments? _____
   _____
   _____ (write on back if needed)

be administered by someone being rated, because that will probably cause employees to be less candid.

The evaluation should *not* be announced to employees in advance. When a day has been selected, set aside a large conference room with tables for writing. Provide a sealed box with a slit on top into which completed evaluations will be dropped.

Ideally, all employees should complete the form together (i.e., in the same room, at the same time). If this is not feasible, the evaluations should be conducted in a series of smaller department groups. By conducting the evaluations all at once (or in small groups in quick succession), you prevent people who have completed the evaluation from influencing those who have not.

Since different employees will be evaluating different managers, individual packets should be assembled for each person completing the evaluation. Within each packet, include the instruction sheet on top, accompanied by the appraisal forms with the appropriate manager's name handwritten in the space at the top of each form.

The packet is then placed in a sealed manila envelope with the employee's name on the outside (since the forms are completed anonymously, this is the only way to verify when all appropriate personnel have completed the evaluation). Under the eye of the designated administrator, the employees are gathered, the envelopes are handed out, and the appraisals are completed in silence. The employees then drop their completed forms, minus the envelope, in the box as they leave.

After all evaluations are complete, the box should be delivered to the president's office (or the outside administrator's office if appropriate) for consolidation into composite ratings for each manager.

The primary purpose of this exercise, if you remember, was to ascertain your *own* rating, so study it carefully. What were your ratings on Questions 2 through 5, compared to the rest of the management team? What were the consolidated responses to Questions 6 through 9, relative to your performance? More importantly, if you want to improve company productivity, what actions are you going to take to improve your performance in any area in which your rating was low (as well as those of other low-rated managers)?

The Challenge of Change

Studying a football play in a team playbook is one thing; adapting it to the next big game and making it work when you are facing the opposing team is quite another. Although I am offering you proven methods, strategies, and techniques to improve your management style, they must be adapted to meet the unique demands of your business and its environment.

And here is where we come full circle. In the last chapter, we modified your business environment to increase productivity. Thus far in this chapter, we have unleashed a process of change within the chief executive, changes to ensure that the company team continues to flourish.

But these changes in the executive may have created the necessity for additional changes within the company—and your employees may resist this new round of changes. You and they need to realize that, if the company is to realize its full potential, change must be a continuous process. Yet people hate change, and the worst thing you can do is force it upon them. So enlist their support and their commitment in helping to bring the additional changes about, because unless they are committed to change, it probably won't happen.

To secure employee commitment to a proposed change, involve your employees. If you win them over first, the change should be a success. Make sure that change is a team effort, not a cause of intramural squabbles between departments. If changes involve pain, be up front about it. And make sure everyone shares equitably in the burden.

A key to inspiring your employee team to embrace and accept change is to convince them by everything you do, as well as by your everyday attitude, that you are wholeheartedly supporting them. To do this, you must have *honesty*. If you don't, all is lost. For example, if employees see you singling out someone in the company and treating him or her shabbily, the others will wonder when it will be their turn to experience your wrath, and you will have lost their respect.

* * *

Now that you've completed the first four "basic" steps in the Macrofruition process, it's time for a transition into the "advanced" steps, where you can leverage the momentum of change to which you have committed into better performance and increased profits.

Part II
The Advanced Steps

Step Five

Remove Barriers and Build Bridges to Profitability

During the first four steps of the Macrofruition process, you took significant strides along the path toward sustained business success. Step Five focuses on smoothing out the roadbed—eliminating barriers that you have not yet addressed and building bridges to achieve enhanced profitability for your company. I'll tackle the barriers first.

A Dozen Managers With Attitude Problems

Over the years I have developed a list of what I consider to be the most potentially devastating business attitudes. These negative attitudes, if embraced by senior managers, represent surefire ways to hobble the growth of a business.

Allow me to introduce you to twelve managers who are inhibiting the growth and success potential of their businesses. The descriptions for each manager incorporate the rationalizations they use to embrace their defective attitudes. I hope your study of the preceding Macrofruition steps has enabled you to spot and to eliminate these destructive approaches to doing business.

- *The Power Monger*. "By keeping all the power for myself, maintaining dictatorial rule, and never asking my employees for suggestions, I ensure that all the glory will be mine. Staff members probably won't do their best, and they won't rush to correct obvious errors or question

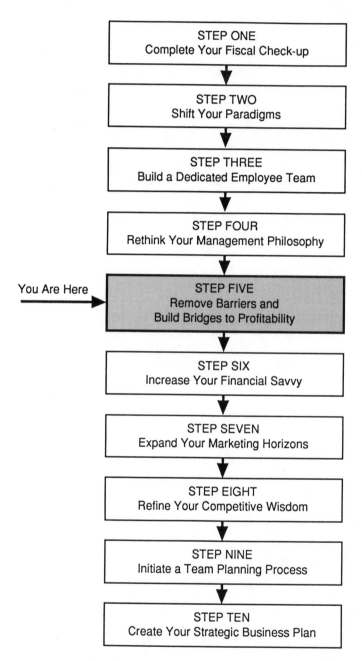

incorrect shipments. If they desert me the minute a better job comes along, I'll just hire and train new workers."

- *The Covert Executive.* "It's best to keep my employees in the dark about the 'big picture' or the company vision. As long as they understand their own jobs and do them well, that's what's important. They really couldn't grasp the importance of my corporate vision anyway, so why bother sharing it with them?"

- *The Immobile Manager.* "Why spend time and money to improve the quality of my products, services, or production processes? What I offered in the past has worked just fine. If my customers are still willing to buy it, that proves they don't need anything better or less expensive. If it ain't broke, why should I spend valuable resources trying to fix it?"

- *The Slave Master.* "I treat my employees like hired hands because that's what they are. I'm the one who makes all the key decisions and takes all the risk. My employees are just tools to get the job done, and I can always find new workers if the old ones wear out. Caring about my employees just diverts time and energy from the job of running my business."

- *The Paranoic.* "It's best to disregard those who want to help me, because they are only using me for their own selfish motives. They couldn't care less whether I succeed; what they are really after is their own success. If I do triumph, they'll take the credit, but if I fail, they'll desert me in an instant."

- *The Procrastinator.* "Keeping the business going is hard enough; I defer difficult decisions because I don't need extra stress. When the really tough problems arise (threatening creditors, abrogated agreements, personnel layoffs), I just put these issues on the back burner. Given enough time, they tend to resolve themselves."

- *The Gambler.* "It's okay to take big risks on new products or services, because that's where the action and excitement are. When pessimists warn that the market is too small, I focus on the joy of creating the product. It's someone else's job to figure out how to sell it."

- *The Omnipotent One.* "I never waste time seeking feedback from my customers. I know more about this business than they do, so it's up to me to determine what's best for them. I'll tell them what the product will do and what it will cost—that's all they need to know. If they have any complaints, they are probably based on a misunderstanding or a misuse of the product anyway, so I usually ignore them."

- *The Ostrich.* "I've got more important things to do than worry about my competition; I see no reason to take valuable time away from running my business just to find out what my competitors are up to. Even if I did learn that they're developing new products, it's too late for me to do anything about it."

- *The Reckless Manager.* "I've spent so much time and money creating my new widget, it's bound to be perfect. There's no need to miss the current selling season just for the sake of some additional testing in the field. Other companies rushing products to market may run into problems, but that's because their products were flawed in the first place. Mine aren't."

- *The Methuselah.* "This product helped me achieve initial success with my company, so I'll keep it going even though sales are dropping off. Sure, every other product or service ever invented had a finite life cycle, but mine is different—it's about to get its second wind. Profits may have been tapering off lately, but, if I keep my original product line open, it will defy the odds and rebound stronger than ever."

- *The Naif.* "I don't worry about the impact of government regulations on my business. Those laws are just a nuisance created by politicians to justify their existence. Environmental protection, worker safety, sexual harassment, and other similar issues aren't really my concern; after all, there are no real problems in my company that I can't handle. Furthermore, regulatory laws are constantly changing, and it's just too expensive to try to keep up with them. If I ever have a problem, I'll have my legislator take care of it. That's what political donations are for, right?"

EXERCISE: Attitude Adjustment

If you found the descriptions above to be nothing more than amusing distractions, fine. But if any of these rationalizations have a familiar ring, you'd better list them in your notebook and make a firm commitment to eliminate your own attitude problems.

There are several other common obstacles to continued growth and profitability. Although these issues are not as potentially life-threatening as the "dirty dozen" just listed, they can result in a significant drain on company morale and on the corporate coffers if they are handled poorly.

Ethics

Ethics is an assemblage of moral principles, a set of values, the internal code of conduct that governs how we act as individuals. Some ethical standards are clear-cut: We know it is wrong to steal from a bank. Others are tougher: Must we tell the store clerk when she hands us too much change?

People who steal, lie, and cheat may be incarcerated because their personal ethics do not conform to society's standards. But would your personal ethics allow you to steal, lie, or cheat if you knew positively that you wouldn't get caught?

All too often we perceive ourselves to be acting ethically because we play by the rules when it comes to the big issues, even though we consistently ignore the small points. We must wake up and realize ethics aren't just a guideline for certain situations; they should be part of the very fabric of our lives.

How ethically are you operating your business? Let's start with a couple of examples that have to do with minor breaches of ethics:

- Suppose you have a written policy that your office copier may not be used for personal business. How would you respond if your neighbor asked if he could use your machine to print a few flyers for his new business venture?

- How do you respond when a fellow business executive asks you to make him a copy of the new word-processing program you just purchased so that he can evaluate it?

If your little actions aren't ethical, your big ones won't be either. For example:

- Suppose you have manufactured a system for a major customer. Under the terms of your contract, you will receive a healthy bonus if it ships tomorrow. However, you are also required to repeat a detailed forty-eight-hour equipment qualification test three times. Your equipment has passed the test twice with flying colors. Do you fudge the results from the third test so that you can ship tomorrow, or do you forgo the bonus?

- You are under pressure from your board of directors to show a profit this quarter on a new program that has been plagued with losses and is making you look bad. But you have another program that is so successful that it is generating buckets of cash. You could easily charge material and time from the unprofitable program against the other program's profits and look like a hero. Would you do it?

• Your company is in the middle of accepting bids for a large number of new office computers. You love pro football, and one of the vendors bidding on the project calls and offers you two box seats to next week's Super Bowl with transportation on his company jet thrown in. Do you accept?

Ethics involves treating everyone—friends, family, financiers, employees, and people from other businesses—according to the same set of rules.

Don't let anyone kid you—poor ethics *always* cost dollars out of someone's pocket. But today the prevailing attitude seems to be, "If I don't see the money coming out of *my own* pocket, I just don't care."

We need to stop kidding ourselves and look at all of our actions critically. Try asking yourself how you would feel if you observed someone else behaving as you are. When you have to start *justifying* or explaining your actions, your ethics are probably faulty.

Ethical violations extend beyond doing something wrong or immoral; they include even the appearance of doing so. The higher up you are in business or in public service, the more relevant this truth. Even if the congressional scandal involving overdrawn accounts at the House bank didn't cost taxpayers a dime, it sent a message around the world regarding the questionable ethics of the elected officials we had in Congress.

Achieving near-term benefits does not justify placing your company in long-term jeopardy. If you don't have squeaky-clean ethics, sooner or later your actions will come back to haunt you—through loss of business and customers, low employee morale and productivity, or lawsuits, all of which can cost your company dearly.

I strongly suggest that you create a written code of ethical conduct for your business. The theme of this code should be that no employee is to

---

EXERCISE: My Ethical Perspective

Write down your perspective of your ethics. Include areas where you are strong and areas where you are weak. List the elements that should be included in a strong code of ethics for your company.

undertake any activity that would negatively affect the company or its assets, another employee, a supplier, a customer, a financier, a competitor, *or any other living being*.

Corporate Manuals

Written manuals—especially personnel and product instruction manuals—are a necessity for every productive business, no matter what its size. Unfortunately, many companies simply don't bother to develop these essential documents.

The Personnel Manual

No matter what the size of your company, if you do not produce a written document outlining in detail your corporate policies, you are asking for trouble in the future. Simply giving a verbal briefing to employees or issuing vague memos about personnel policies is bound to lead to conflict.

Here's an example. I was recently contacted by the president of a midwestern start-up service business. The preceding spring, he had instituted the company's first paid vacation policy. Then, during the last week in December, he had reminded employees that unused vacation days couldn't be carried into the new year.

I say "reminded" because, although there was no written record of the vacation policy, the CEO insisted that he had verbally informed employees of this feature of the policy when it was instituted in March. According to employees, though, no such information had been conveyed. They protested loudly against the policy, and it was rescinded.

The moral of this story is clear: Put your policies on paper! You have enough confrontations with the outside world; you don't need internal conflicts. By producing a personnel manual that clearly and simply states company policies, you can avoid misunderstanding and resentment.

Think of your personnel manual as your silent sentinel. Its purpose is to help your employees make the right decisions when you aren't around and to avoid any potential charges of favoritism or unfair treatment.

There are a number of publications available to assist you in producing an effective personnel manual. But you can make a good start on your own.

Begin by putting every one of your company policies in writing, with appropriate detail. Keeping the wording simple; you don't want the manual to read like a legal brief. Ensure that policies are clearly stated by having several people review your first draft and identify confusing language or passages.

I recommend that your manual include at least the following: a description of policies on working hours, breaks, tardiness, vacations, and holidays; a detailed explanation of benefits, including any costs to employees; a summary of employee review and wage adjustment cycles; and a description of the length of the probationary period for new employees. Also, discuss actions that may result in reprimands or dismissal; the company's layoff policy; how employee grievances are handled; and requirements for travel, customer meetings, and trade shows.

Once you have included all these items, add any other company policies you've developed. You might also consider including your company's vision statement (and/or list of goals) on the front page of the manual, along with a strong statement about customer service, so that every employee knows what the company is striving to achieve.

Each page in the manual should be marked with a date, revision, and page number to ensure that employees have a copy of the latest version and aren't missing any pages. Also, mark manuals as "Company Confidential," not to be shared outside the company.

Update your personnel manual at specific times each year, and provide each employee with a new, revised manual. Add a black vertical stripe in the margin next to each paragraph that has been changed or added since the previous revision. This will help to focus employees' awareness on the policy changes made since the last manual was issued.

Always meet with employees to explain significant changes in policy (for minor changes, a memorandum will suffice). And give them the opportunity to verbalize their dissatisfaction with the change at the time that you notify them, to avoid having them vent their wrath later in unproductive ways.

The Product Instruction Manual

Put yourself in your customer's shoes for a moment. How many times have you purchased a product, only to find that it comes with an unintelligible instruction manual that reads as if it were written as a hasty afterthought?

Consumers aren't overly demanding in this department. They want a product manual that will accomplish two things: (1) let them set up and use the product easily, and (2) enable them to find reference topics quickly.

One of the biggest mistakes that manufacturers make is to spend significant resources to build a quality product and then to skimp when it comes to the instruction manual. Buyers may purchase a product as a result of effective marketing, but, once they get it home, if they can't master it immediately, they will believe the product is inferior—guilty by association—no matter how good it really is.

A high-quality manual can generate repeat sales, even if you have a mediocre product, because it shows that you care about your customers. But a poorly written manual guarantees you will lose repeat sales of your product and can doom referral sales.

Recently I purchased a replacement barbecue grill for my patio. It came disassembled, and I followed the instruction manual, step by step. The manual was so poorly written that I had to disassemble the main grill in Step 18 after assembling it in Step 10, just so I could attach a side warmer cover.

The product design wasn't faulty, but the order of assembly was. It was obvious that the instruction manual had never been tested. I'll remember this the next time I go shopping for a grill and will probably purchase a different brand. And you can bet I'd never recommend this product to a friend.

Some of the most notorious instruction manual offenders are computer software manufacturers. Programming gurus may know all the intimate details of their software, but they write their manuals as if they were dictionaries, focusing on program features rather than on how to use the program. Consumers don't want definitions; they want a user-friendly presentation on the typical assembly or installation and use of the product.

Some technical wizards also omit basic points in their manuals. Perhaps they are too close to the product, or perhaps they forget that consumers don't have their level of understanding. Whatever the reason, the outcome is customer frustration and alienation. Some companies add insult to injury by charging customers who call their customer service hotline for help in deciphering their instructions.

Three years ago, I purchased an expensive sales lead tracking program. It came with a 780-page manual that focused on features, rather than on how to use the program. One day, I accidentally touched a seldom-used key on my keyboard, and a special screen that made it easier to track my key clients appeared. I called the company to ask about my discovery. The response I got was, "Oh, good, you found the key screen. You're really lucky because we forgot to put it in the manual."

Here's how to ensure that your product instruction manuals are user-friendly: Give both your product and your manual to nontechnical people who don't work for your company, and have them evaluate it without your help. They will find the weaknesses fast. Don't try to explain away the problems; fix them, instead.

Here is another helpful hint: Anxious customers tend to ignore lengthy manuals. I recommend that you provide a short "quick start" manual to help get the buyer started, as well as a larger reference manual (again focused on operation, not features) so that the user can later study a particular function in more depth.

Mastering Meetings

Do you find yourself constantly running behind schedule with your meetings? If you answered yes to this question, chances are your employees are frustrated because of the valuable time they spend waiting for you to show up for those meetings.

Internal meetings tend to be the bane of many businesses. Since you can't live without them, I suggest you find a way to make them work for you, rather than against you.

You can begin by looking at the number of meetings you have scheduled. Ask yourself if all those meetings are really necessary.

For example, do you really need a staff meeting every Monday morning, or would every other Monday morning be satisfactory? Must you personally attend every meeting? Could you combine some of the meetings you now have? Could you eliminate others in favor of brief telephone discussions or short written reports?

There are some meetings you can't eliminate. But you can ensure that they are as brief and productive as possible. Insisting on written agendas is a good starting point.

I require a written agenda prior to every meeting I attend. My rule is: no agenda, no meeting. If it's not a regularly scheduled meeting (such as a staff meeting), I expect the agenda to include a brief statement of purpose.

Let your employees know that wasteful meetings will no longer be tolerated in your company. Begin each meeting by restating the purpose and the agenda of the meeting. Be merciless with any deviations.

If a meeting strays from the written agenda, it is the duty of the meeting leader to bring the meeting back into focus. If there is insufficient time to complete discussion of the agenda items or if a relevant new topic arises, the leader should schedule a follow-up meeting, rather than continue with the discussion.

If you allow a meeting to drag on beyond its stated time limit, you risk alienating those people who have prepared for the meeting that follows—to which you are going to be late. (And once a meeting is scheduled, you should cancel or reschedule only if there is a compelling reason to do so.)

Occasionally, there is a valid reason for a meeting to run slightly long (with the emphasis on "slightly"). For this reason, I always have my secretary schedule a reasonable buffer on my calendar. For example, if I have a one-hour meeting scheduled at 9:00 A.M., I won't schedule another meeting until 11:00 A.M.

If you relax your meeting schedule and never let meetings diverge too far from their stated agendas and time frames, both you and your staff can breathe a sigh of relief. You will be the master of your meetings, and not vice versa.

Swelling and Shrinking the Business

Successful businesses grow and shrink in size, expanding when faced with increased demand and downsizing during tough times. Whether you are expanding or downsizing your business, you need to do so in a constructive manner in order to minimize potential traumatic effects.

Expanding the Company

You shouldn't hesitate to expand your work force when you are certain that growth will continue at a steady pace. However, if your growing company is small and cash is tight, you must augment your work force wisely, because you can't afford to have any duds on the payroll.

Consider hiring additional staff through temporary employment agencies. You'll pay more on an hourly basis, but you will not have to deal with tax records or withholding, and you will avoid benefit and unemployment costs. Furthermore, if a temporary employee doesn't work out, you can just tell the temporary agency to send someone else. If the employee does work out, you can negotiate with the agency to hire him or her permanently after you've paid the agency for a period of time (usually three to five weeks). If your temporary agency won't allow you to hire away its temps, plenty of other agencies will, since you could represent a significant source of business for them if they treat you well.

I suggest you develop an ongoing relationship with a sound temporary agency by which, even if a qualified applicant walks in your door, you send him or her to your temporary service partner. It's like the old saying: "You scratch my back, and I'll scratch yours."

One final caution: Make sure your growth is not temporary or seasonal before you make permanent hires.

If you have a manufacturing business, consider adding temporary production staff with a "mothers' shift." I did this successfully with my first business. I reasoned there were many qualified women out there who had left the work force to raise a family. I offered a special shift that started at 9:00 A.M. (after the kids were in school) and ended at 3:00 P.M. (before the school day ended). When there is a drop in the work load, such workers accept layoff and recall far more easily than full-timers. If you treat them well, they'll become a loyal addition to your staff.

Another idea for manufacturers is to establish a "cottage system" of independent subcontractors—people who pick up the raw materials from your facility, assemble your widgets in their own homes, and return them to you, getting paid on a piece-work basis. Because such workers are independent contractors, you don't have to deal with tax withholding or provide company benefits.

Two areas of caution, if you elect to use this type of system:

1. Since by law you can't issue directives to independent subcontractors, you need to have some kind of bonus system that pays them extra for superior work, thus ensuring they won't return with sloppily built widgets.
2. You need to consult with an experienced business-law attorney. The government gets touchy on the subject of independent subcontractors. If the IRS believes you have set up a sham subcontracting program in an illegal attempt to avoid paying withholding and social security taxes, watch out.

Have your attorney draft a form for your subcontractors to sign. The form should state that they are in business for themselves, that they own and maintain all their own tools and equipment, and that they are willing to contract with other companies for the same type of work.

Downsizing the Company

There are a number of events that may necessitate the reduction of your work force, such as an economic downturn, negative market changes, or the elimination of product lines. When it's time for the scalpel, you must perform the surgery with the least amount of pain.

Downsizing can be a traumatic experience for employees, and it's no picnic for management; having to lay off good employees is never an easy task.

However, resist the temptation to delay necessary layoffs just because you don't want to hurt people. If employees suspect a layoff is coming, you will only hurt them more by inaction.

During a downsizing, you must take great pains to be perceived as fair. Keep your most effective employees, not necessarily the most senior. If you choose to keep people on the payroll solely on the basis of seniority or friendship or for some reason other than ability, you will lose credibility and the respect of your employees.

If you have six employees in marketing and two must be laid off, consider the quality of the group that will remain after the layoffs. You will need the four employees who can best work together to handle an increased post-layoff workload.

In executing layoffs, you as the CEO should take an active part in meeting with employees face to face. Resist the temptation to write a memo to your employees or to pass the baton to subordinates too early in the process. *You* must face your employees, explaining the situation and answering their questions. You owe them that much.

When my first company had grown to fifty-five employees, I had to initiate the largest layoff of my executive career. Because my biggest customer refused to pay a $200,000 debt, I ran out of cash and was forced to lay off forty employees until I could resolve the crisis.

I called all my employees together and explained why the layoff was necessary and how we had tried to avoid it. I thanked them for their hard work and told them how sorry I was. I let them know when the layoffs would begin, and I gave them my best estimate as to how long they would last. I also tried to explain the process we used to decide who would be laid off.

Then I answered their questions. I concluded by telling them that their supervisors would be providing them with specific details, adding that they could see me if they had any further questions. I made sure all the supervisors were well briefed about each employee's situation so that they could offer advice about where to turn for short-term benefits (unemployment compensation) and assistance with job searches.

Although my employees weren't happy about the prospect of being laid off, they understood the company's situation. Ultimately, the crisis was resolved; within six months every employee was rehired.

People tend to be fair with you if you treat them fairly. When you find it necessary to downsize your company, do so in a rational, responsible, and compassionate manner. And, by the way, if your cutbacks are the result of cash flow problems, the remaining managers (including the CEO) should take significant pay cuts.

Building Bridges to Enhanced Profitability

When you are satisfied that you have eliminated or at least minimized any barriers to future growth and profitability, it's time to turn your attention to those activities that have the greatest potential to bring about increased profits.

The Line-Item Veto

The concept of the line-item veto involves giving consideration to modifying, subcontracting, or eliminating marginal portions of your business operations. To determine if a line-item veto is warranted, take an in-depth look at each of your products or services. What is the contribution of each to your bottom line? How about each one's return on investment? Could any portion of your assembly or sales processes be handled more profitably outside your company? Could other activities be subcontracted to outside firms (such as advertising, accounting, or payroll) to increase your bottom line profits?

Tracking Maximum Profits

These are important questions, but chances are your present accounting system doesn't allow you to answer them. If your business is like most companies, your accounting system is set up to track expenses by department. This yields what I refer to as *function-centered tracking*, which traces costs incurred within each major function (such as marketing, sales, and administration) within your organization.

Take a look at Figure 5-1. A representative organization chart is overlaid with gray ovals, indicating typical expense tracking. You can define total costs for various functional areas: marketing and sales, administration, engineering, and production. Add them all together, and you have total expenses.

This is the way most companies handle expense tracking. The problem is that you have no idea how much each functional area is contributing to the corporate coffers.

Figure 5-1. Function-centered tracking.

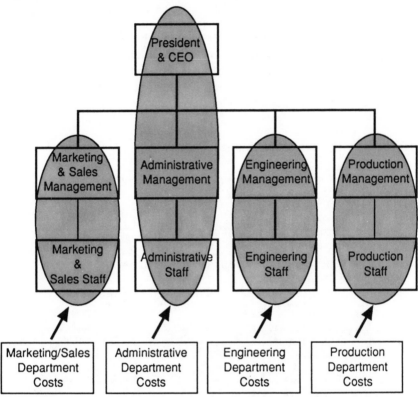

If you want to enhance your profitability in the long run, you must either improve the performance of your low-producing product lines or eliminate them. To do this, you need to be able to "look down the pipeline" of each product, determining its contribution to overall profits. This is accomplished by changing your accounting system to *product-centered tracking*.

Product-centered tracking involves allocating the total costs incurred in each department to your various product lines. To track costs in this way, have each department employee (whether hourly or salaried) allocate time to specific products each month. Have the accounting department determine how to allocate other expenses, such as phone calls and brochures, among products.

Certain expenses, such as administrative costs, can be allocated on the basis of how many employees work on each product. For example, if a company has twenty people working on Product A, thirty on Product B, forty on Product C, and ten in administration, then allocate two-ninths of administration costs to A, three-ninths to B, and four-ninths to C.

Once you modify your accounting system to track costs accordingly, a new image will emerge, and you will be able to look at the true costs related to each product line. Figure 5-2 shows such a system for a

Figure 5-2. Product-centered tracking.

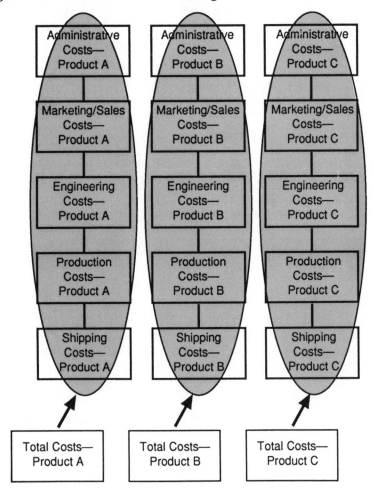

company with three product lines. This company can take the total sales for Product A and deduct the total costs for Product A, thereby determining exactly what A contributes to profits.

Ideally, you want the cost percentage in each product line to be as low as possible relative to the revenue percentage. At the very least, it shouldn't be far above the revenue percentage. For example, if Product A represents 45 percent of overall revenues and 40 percent of overall costs, you will probably be satisfied. But if you determine that B represents 60 percent of costs but only 30 percent of revenues, you had better do something fast. That "something" might be internal streamlining, outsourcing, or eliminating the product line.

Internal Streamlining

If your individual product line revenue and cost percentages are out of line, you must determine what area of the pipeline is costing too much. Look at the percentages of administration costs versus revenues, then marketing costs versus revenues, then engineering costs versus revenues, and so on. If you find that marketing is the most significant contributor to cost of a particular product, redistribute the total marketing budget so that fewer marketing dollars are allocated to that product and more are spread among the other products.[1] If production costs are the most significant contributor, strive for greater production process efficiency.

Outsourcing

If you cannot achieve any further improvements internally and your costs are still too high, give serious consideration to farming out certain elements of your production and marketing processes. This might involve subcontracting assembly of circuit boards or utilizing an outside telemarketing firm, advertising agency, or printing firm. Look at the true costs of individual activities (for example, all the fringe benefits and additional costs added to wages). If a process can be handled less expensively outside the company, move it there.

---

1. Note that, during a promotion for an individual product line, marketing expenses may be higher for the short term, and no further action is necessary. However, over a longer period, of one or two quarters, the percentage should be much more realistic. If it is not, action should be taken.

Eliminating Products

If you have investigated all other avenues to no avail, give serious consideration to dropping the product line. If for some reason you cannot do this, then at least pare back the budget for that miserly product line and pass these funds to the most profitable line.

Waking Up to Total Quality Management

Are you willing to consider a radical change in the way you do business, if the result is a stronger bottom line? Unless you have been living in a cave for the past several years, you have probably heard about Total Quality Management (TQM). However, chances are you still don't know what it is.

TQM has come to refer to a broad class of activities to improve business productivity. These activities are based on the premise that those people closest to the work know the best way to improve the performance of that portion of the business. Through a period of training that typically begins with senior executives and spreads downward throughout the organization, employees are empowered to make these changes.

Many American companies still don't take quality seriously. One indication of this: In a May 1992 *Wall Street Journal* survey of international companies, 40 percent of the U.S. companies surveyed used *profit* as the primary criterion for determining compensation for senior managers. But fewer than 20 percent of those same companies used *quality* (including customer satisfaction) as a criterion.

By failing to focus on quality, these companies may be unwittingly sacrificing long-term benefits for short-term profits. Many companies currently in the process of dying may still be turning a profit. If they don't pay attention to quality now, these businesses will never keep up with their higher-quality competitors in the future.

Why have U.S. companies taken so long to accept TQM? First of all, there is no standard cookbook approach for implementation. Furthermore, TQM is a bit of an enigma because it has no universal definition or plan of implementation. Although it was originally developed for manufacturing firms, it can be applied to any type of business, including service businesses. How a company institutes TQM depends on a number of critical factors, such as the company's goals, the composition of the employee staff, and the dynamics of the markets it is addressing.

The basic philosophy of TQM is to make every product or process, not just good, but the best it can possibly be.

In the past, American executives tended to equate quality with a cadre of inspectors. Responsibility for quality rested with the quality department or the quality inspector who checked the final product to make sure it met the company's standards.

Under TQM, quality is everybody's business. TQM requires all employees to "design" quality into the very fabric of the business, from the actual production of a product or service to its marketing. It also determines how employees deal with suppliers, distributors, and, especially, with customers.

Properly administered, TQM inspires all employees to give strict attention to every detail of their work and how it can be improved. Typical results include the elimination of unnecessary steps in production processes and the refinement of procedures to save time.

Such results can be dramatic. For example, Electric Controls in Watertown, Massachusetts, modified the design and assembly of its industrial control systems and slashed delivery times from twelve weeks to less than one week, using the principles of TQM.

Total Quality Management can also be applied to service businesses. In such cases, the focus is often on achieving superior levels of customer satisfaction. Here, too, the end result of TQM efforts can be impressive. Alaska Airlines continues to attract customers by offering more legroom and other creature comforts. The company spends double the U.S. average for airline meals, serving fresh fruit and entrees like fresh salmon in coach class. Alaska keeps in touch with its customers by conducting periodic consumer focus groups and by asking frequent flyers how the airline can improve.

As the 1990s began, Alaska Airlines expanded its service to the entire West Coast of the United States and to Mexico. The company's revenues continued to grow by more than 24 percent annually during the early 1990s, a time when other airlines were drowning in a sea of red ink.

Under TQM, quality is measured by customers' satisfaction with your product or service. Consider this sobering statistic: 68 percent of the customers who stop doing business with a company do so because of poor service.[2]

Total Quality Management focuses, not on making single dramatic improvements in quality, but in making a host of small, continuous

2. From *Creating the Environment for Total Quality Management* (Chicago: A.T. Kearney, 1991). This is a pamphlet available exclusively from A. T. Kearney.

improvements—what the Japanese call *kaizen*. Such seemingly small steps add up to major improvements. An improvement of only one-tenth of 1 percent in quality each week achieved by applying TQM results in an increase of more than 5 percent each year and 26 percent after five years. And that's real progress!

TQM principles require a radical change in management as power is shifted to lower levels of employees. Executives in a TQM business are less involved in autocratic management and more involved in setting goals, empowering their employees to work more efficiently and productively, and providing the tools employees need to do their jobs.

Under TQM, employees are an integral part of the creation of new products and services. Employees typically form teams and become the "experts" who solve problems in their own work areas. Under TQM programs, bonus systems are usually created for all employees as an additional incentive to improve quality.

Giving authority and responsibility for quality to the employees who are closest to the action, rather than to a distant quality inspector, can result in sometimes startling improvements in quality. Here's an example: At one time, a division of Hewlett-Packard, the electronics giant, had a circuit board defect rate of four per thousand. Management sought help from its engineers to solve the problem; they managed to reduce the defect rate by 50 percent, to two per thousand.

Then management asked the assembly workers who produced the boards to attack the problem. The result? These front-line workers reduced the defect rate by an additional 99.9 percent, to two per *million*!

Total Quality Management represents a powerful method of improving quality and profitability. But it is not without problems. For one thing, management may expect dramatic results from TQM virtually overnight. This is unrealistic; it takes time to change from an old, familiar way of doing business. Furthermore, some insecure executives may be reluctant to give up their power to other employees, but they must if TQM is going to work. Finally, TQM requires time and money for training and for establishing a series of internal Process Action Teams to assess various operations for potential improvement.

Historically, the most successful TQM programs have involved a strong, visible, ongoing involvement by all senior executives, coupled with a companywide awareness of strategic goals and an emphasis on simplifying processes and helping customers.

TQM requires an ongoing, almost religious zeal on the part of the chief executive, who plots the course for others to follow. If the CEO isn't fully committed and doesn't understand and embrace TQM concepts, and if he or she doesn't constantly communicate TQM leadership to the rest of the company, the TQM initiative within that company is probably doomed to fail.

Don't try to rush into an implementation of TQM, and don't expect that TQM will solve major problems immediately. Instead, I suggest you study TQM thoroughly before attempting implementation and set a realistic timetable, because you will be undertaking a fundamental change in the way you run your company.

Whether your business is in manufacturing, retail, or service or whether you work in the public sector, TQM can add horsepower to your company, its employees, and its bottom line. Whether it's the way you serve eggs to a customer or help someone book an airline flight, or fix people's cars, you should learn to make Total Quality Management part of your company's creed.

For some excellent reading sources to get you started on the path to Total Quality Management, see Appendix A at the back of the book.

EXERCISE: My TQM Potential

As you analyze your company from the perspective of this TQM overview, what areas within your business could benefit most from immediate application of TQM principles: design, marketing, sales, customer service? Is it sufficiently intriguing that you want to learn more regarding the implementation?

Recharging Your Batteries

Being at the helm of a dynamic business can be a rewarding, yet draining, experience. No matter how much you believe the company needs you, you must take time off and spend quality time with family and friends, away from the business environment. The changes you have initiated or are contemplating in your company as a result of this book are a step in the right direction, because empowering others should allow you the freedom to disengage from the rigors of the chief executive's office without guilt.

Cashing in the Chips

Even if profits are still flowing in, if you are no longer having fun, if you have lost the zest for the challenges within your business, or if you have become complacent and content to rest on past achievements, you should seriously consider passing the baton to a successor. You are probably inhibiting your company's growth. If you cannot (or will not) change that attitude, you should be using the pages of this book to help you make the difficult decision of how best to pass the mantle of company leadership to a successor.

If this is the decision facing you, realize that, in this all-important last act as chief executive, you will be launching the company on a new course, one that will have a major impact on you and on those you leave behind. Think carefully about the potential consequences of your decision. For example, if you choose the buyout option that gives you the greatest amount of money but also results in the dismantling of the company as you know it, are the extra dollars really worth it?

You will still have concern for the direction of the company after you depart, so make your decision with care. You will be judged by your employees as to the wisdom of your decision; approach it with dignity.

*   *   *

The activities outlined in this chapter, if pursued with diligence, should have a pronounced positive effect on your company's income and expenses. In the next chapter, we show how you can further enhance profitability by making the most of your existing and potential financial resources.

Step Six

Increase Your Financial Savvy

Most of the Macrofruition steps you've taken thus far will have a positive effect on your company's financial health. However, there are still some specific financial pointers and pitfalls to be addressed. These are covered in Step Six of the Macrofruition process.

As part of this step, I'll show you how to make the most of your fiscal resources, both internal and external. Armed with this information, you will be able to generate a strong fiscal game plan to ensure the continued financial health of your company.

The Importance of Financial Planning

The only time many executives do any serious financial planning and evaluation is during the week before their annual pilgrimage to their bankers' office. This is a mistake. Finances aren't something you should think about once a year; if you want to ensure the continued growth and profitability of your business, you had better keep track of them at all times.

I suggest you start by developing two sets of financial plans: short-term and long-term.

Your short-term financial plan should focus on steps that must be taken to achieve bottom-line profit objectives for this year and the next. These steps will probably center around minimizing expenses and maximizing orders.

Your long-term plan should facilitate continued strong financial growth three to five years into the future. Achieving long-term growth

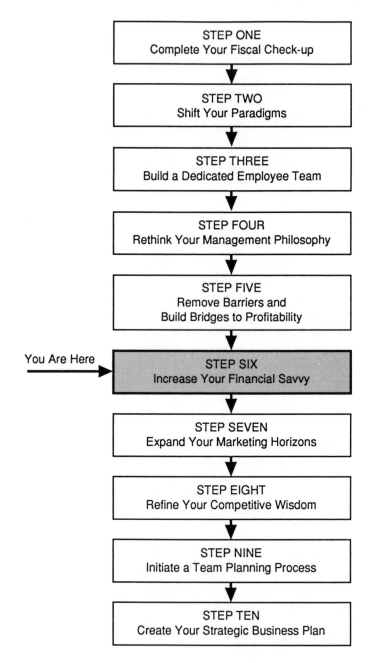

objectives will probably involve major projects, such as establishing a new line of products or automating an assembly process.

You will likely need capital in order to reach your long-term financial goals, and possibly even your short-term objectives. Before discussing the variety of capital sources available to you, let's consider your business from the perspective of potential financiers.

A Few Words About Financiers

Financiers will never become as excited about your business as you are, because you don't share the same goal. Your goal is the growth and profitability of your company. Their goal is to make money by investing prudently and at an acceptable level of risk.

No matter how exciting your company's product or service, the less experience your management team appears to have, the more risk your company will pose to financiers. Given the choice between backing companies with 1. a *superior* product produced or marketed by *inexperienced* managers or 2. a *mediocre* product produced or marketed by *experienced* managers, financiers—whether lenders or equity investors—inevitably choose the mediocre product with experienced managers, because the odds for success (i.e., return on investment) are much greater. (Come to think of it, maybe that's why we see so many mediocre products out there.)

Although both value managerial experience over product, debt and equity financiers often look at your company from different perspectives. Bankers, who lend debt capital, look for low risk and usually avoid early-stage companies unless the owners have a great deal of collateral or can qualify for a Small Business Administration (SBA) loan (in which case the SBA provides the additional collateral required). For this reason, bank loans are typically utilized for expansion and for acquisition of inventory by existing businesses.

Equity financiers, by contrast, often fund "earlier"-stage, higher-risk companies, but they also expect far greater returns on their investments. And they may want to guide you in your business decisions by sitting on your board of directors (a plus for you, since you thereby gain access to their wealth of business experience).

Most financial packages for businesses are a combination of equity and debt, even when all of the funding comes from equity financiers. These financiers usually want to own some portion of the stock, but they also want a part of the package to consist of a loan, thus providing them with some near-term cash return on their investment in the form of interest payments.

Figure 6-1 shows the typical sources of capital for various uses. We first explore the subject of debt financing. Then we examine the variety of equity capital sources that can be tapped.

Debt Financing

Your Banker's Perspective

Once an early-stage company is several years old and has advanced beyond the start-up tremors, it can be assigned to one of three categories, according to its performance: winner, norm, or loser.

Winners are those companies that are profitable and continuing to grow. Norms are companies that are just breaking even, neither growing nor shrinking. Losers are companies that are sustaining substantial losses. Bankers are willing to lend capital either to winners or norms, assuming their funds are protected by adequate collateral. (Obviously, no financier is interested in the loser category.)

Bankers are businesspeople, and, like you, they need to make a profit. If they don't thoroughly know or understand *you*, your business philosophy, and your business, the process of getting their approval for a loan is far more difficult because they equate their lack of understanding with higher risk. All of your ongoing dealings with your bankers should therefore be focused on minimizing their perceived risk.

Figure 6-1. Uses of debt and equity capital.

Debt Capital	Equity Capital
▪ To expand markets when company has solid, positive cash flow	▪ To expand markets when company lacks sufficient positive cash flow
▪ For receivables/inventory financing or operating capital for profitable company	▪ For receivables/inventory financing or operating capital for unprofitable company
▪ For new equipment in established company	▪ For new equipment in early-stage company
▪ To offset seasonal cash flow shortfall	▪ For research and development or for new product development

Getting to Know Your Bankers

To familiarize bankers with you and your company, try approaching them *before* you need the next round of debt capital. Provide them with financial statements, and invite them to business briefings and facility tours well in advance of filing your loan request. This strategy will ensure that your bank executives understand *what you do* and *how well you do it*, so you will not have to overcome the additional hurdle of educating them during your next loan application process.

How long has it been since you invited your banker on a tour of your facilities? If there have been significant changes affecting sales, productivity, or profits since his or her last visit, it's time to extend the invitation again.

Even if you are meeting all your loan payments and the company is in good health, never take your bankers for granted or wait until you have a new loan pending to extend to them an invitation to visit. Such an invitation on the heels of a loan application may be cause for suspicion on their part. Invite them during times of minimal activity between your company and their institution so they perceive you have no ulterior motive.

Your bankers deal with many businesses. Over time, they may forget some of the specifics that make yours unique and a low financial risk, so never neglect the opportunity to reeducate them; this could be one of the best investments in time you'll ever make.

Applying for a Loan

The Loan Process

The typical bank loan is for a specific project, such as the addition of a product line. Because bankers want absolute minimum risk, they want to see a project plan covering the next twelve to eighteen months, instead of a detailed business plan.[1] Bankers aren't concerned about your company's performance five years into the future; they want to be assured that you can repay your loan within the next year or year and a half.

You should be prepared to pledge significant collateral against your loan—at least 150 percent or more of the amount sought, depending on your banker's perception of risk.

---

1. The only exception is if you are applying for a start-up (or SBA) loan, in which case loan officials will want to see a full formal business plan.

The process of applying for your bank loan is a marketing task. You must sell three factors to your bank: the wisdom of the project, the strength of your business, and, most important, your ability as chief executive. If your banker has confidence in all three, this may even offset a weak balance sheet.

Initially, concentrate on selling your project to your loan officer. Only an enthusiastic loan officer can effectively champion your project before the infamous loan committee. (In most cases, the loan officer knows what the answer will be before he or she takes it to the committee. If you sense a hesitancy on the banker's part before your application has been acted upon, ask if there is something you should be doing to improve your chances for a positive decision.)

When you brief your loan officer, make sure you include a clear, factual analysis of the market, one that clearly demonstrates why you will succeed. A mere pledge on your part to work hard is not enough to loosen your banker's pursestrings. Your financiers need to see evidence of a significant demand in the market, coupled with your ability to manage an ongoing growth business.

In your banker's analysis of your request, three broad concerns will be addressed:

1. The company, senior executives, or major stockholders must have sufficient assets available to be pledged as collateral for the loan.
2. The bank must believe the proposed project will generate sufficient additional cash flow to repay the loan, with a generous margin of safety.
3. The management team's experience must be sufficient to provide the lender a feeling of confidence.

It is up to you to provide your banker with the details to satisfy these concerns. Arm your banker with the detailed information needed to prove yours is a low-risk, well-managed business, and you'll stand a better chance of getting your money and building a strong, long-lasting banking relationship.

Loan Rejection

Suppose you submitted your loan request and were turned down. What would your response be?

Many business executives respond to rejection by making an awkward exit, fuming, resolving never to do business with that bank again and determined to tell their business associates to do likewise. But if you react this way, what have you gained? And what have you learned? Absolutely nothing.

The bank rejected you for a reason. What was it? Use your bank's rejection to gain additional information from your banker.

Ask what factors led to the bank's negative decision. Did you fail to provide enough information? Does your banker perceive your business to be too high a risk? If so, why?

Never turn your back and walk away from a negative response. Learn from the experience, pinpoint your weaknesses, and correct your deficiencies before trying again—whether you change bankers or not.

Developing Pro Formas

If, when you apply for additional funding, your banker marks down your revenue forecasts, there's a reason. Perhaps you have consistently overstated revenue projections in the past. To find out whether this is the case, compare your projections for the last few years (as originally presented to your banker) against the results you actually achieved. If your actual results were consistently worse than projections, your banker has every reason to react as he or she did, and you had best revise future projections accordingly.

If you find this is not the problem, there are other possibilities to consider. Maybe your projections seem too optimistic when compared with typical growth patterns for companies in your industry. Maybe your operating expenses have increased beyond prudent levels. Or perhaps your banker believes you are not taking other factors, such as a looming recession, into account.

Of course, the best way to find out the real reason your banker marked down your revenue projections is to ask. Then listen carefully to your banker's response, because there is a weakness you need to correct. Business executives tend to believe that no one understands their business better than they do. However, in many instances, your banker *does* understand the *financial* side of your business better than you do, so pay attention.

There is a way to avoid markdowns in the future, while at the same time showing your banker that you understand the impact of outside forces on your business. The next time you assemble a new set of pro forma projections for your financiers, don't prepare just one set, prepare three of them.

Start by developing your usual set of pro formas, and label these your "nominal" projections. These represent what you realistically expect your business to achieve.

Then prepare a set of "best case" projections, assuming you secure some big orders you hadn't expected to win or your major competitor closes shop or your products receive some intensive positive recognition. This version should represent, not pipe dreams, but possible scenarios that were not considered in your nominal projections. This set of projections should include increases in staffing and other expenses associated with the projected revenue increases.

Finally, prepare a set of "worst case" projections that take into account scenarios that, although not probable, could have a significant negative impact on your business if they were to occur. For example, what would happen if you lost a major order, if your largest customer declared bankruptcy, or if you had a fire or a severe supply problem? In addition to showing the loss of revenues that would result, this set of projections should show the associated reductions in staffing, inventory, and expenses.

Approach your banker with all three sets of pro formas, explaining that the nominal set represents the results you expect to achieve, with the other two covering worst-case and best-case contingencies. By doing so, you will convey the image of an experienced financial executive to your banker, who may elect to accept your projections at face value.

Keeping Communication Lines Open

During your annual financial conference, you may develop a vague, uneasy feeling that subtle, negative changes are taking place in your banker's attitude. Watch out for the following danger signals: your banker discusses business politely, instead of with the enthusiasm of past meetings; your loan officer is hesitant about expanding your line of credit; your banker suggests you might want to consider raising additional equity; he or she starts asking for more details about the business, devalues your sales projections, or suggests you slow down your company's growth.

All of these responses reflect the banker's concern that your company is becoming too much of a risk to maintain the status quo. You had better respond to these concerns, even if that simply means keeping your banker better informed about the course of your business.

If your performance and relationship with your banker have been less than admirable, you may want to sit in judgment on yourself to see if you have provided your banker with all the information he or she needs to be assured that your company is continuing to head in the right direction. If your bankers believe you will succeed, they will work with you, but, if they believe you will fail, they must cut their losses.

If you believe your company is still sound and your banker doesn't, then you have failed to do a good job of communicating. If your banker's judgment seems harsh, it's not just because of you; rather, it's the cumulative result of your banker's past dealings with deceitful business borrowers.

How can you set yourself apart from these dishonest debtors? First, provide your banker with frequent financial statements, as well as a written general manager's report detailing your company's performance, projecting future results, and explaining the causes of any downturns.

Submit these documents at least quarterly; monthly is even better. You want your banker to believe you are doing the best possible job of running your business. To accomplish this, you must provide your banker with hard facts, not propaganda, hopes, and pipe dreams.

Second, when your business encounters turbulence, don't try to distance yourself from your financial partner. Keep your banker posted even during difficult times. If you approach your banker needing an emergency cash infusion because of some major negative event you have kept secret until now, he or she will rightly wonder what other information you have deliberately withheld. And you are not likely to get the needed cash.

The best way to reveal bad news to your banker is to explain three critical elements: 1. the nature and extent of the negative results; 2. why they occurred (don't pass the blame); and 3. what steps you are taking to ensure that the misstep will not happen again. These points can be covered in a section of your general manager's report.

When things are not going well and your banker starts talking tough, either you have failed to provide the above information or your business really is in a terminal nose dive. Choosing to ignore your financier is a sure way to guarantee the destruction of your business.

Swallow your pride. No matter how shaky your company's situation, continue to talk to your banker. If you have failed to provide relevant information (even if this information may be a poor reflection on you), explain the situation, and ask for your banker's recommendation.

Your banker may require an additional infusion of equity capital before granting any further loans. This means that the bank is looking for an indication that your business is sufficiently sound to attract other outside investors. If confronted with this request, you may have to bring in additional equity partners. This means putting together a written plan and approaching individuals about a private investment. (See the discussion on creative equity capital sources later in this chapter for suggestions about possible sources of additional funding.)

Equity Financing

Sooner or later, the growth of your company may require that serious consideration be given to bringing in outside equity investors. Equity capitalists come in two flavors: professional *venture capital funds*, which invest institutional capital, primarily in technology-driven businesses, and *private investors*, who typically invest their own capital in young companies.

Venture Capital

Unlike bankers, venture capitalists focus only on companies that are clear winners (even though fate steps in, and usually less than 50 percent of their investments make money). In a typical venture capitalist's portfolio of investments, 20 percent will be total failures, 50 percent will just break even, 20 percent will make a slight profit, and 10 percent will be superstars. These investors won't invest a dime in your business unless they believe it has the potential to be one of their superstars.

To compensate for the mediocre showing of the rest of their portfolio, venture capitalists will expect the rate of return on their investment in you to average more than 25 percent per year. And the poorer your company's performance when you approach them, the greater the ownership stake they will demand.

If you have a start-up company, be prepared to give away from 50 to 80 percent of your company to venture capitalists. At the other extreme, if you approach venture capitalists after you are already profitable, you may have to give up only 10 to 20 percent of the business to receive the same amount of capital.

Because of the due diligence cost of verifying and preparing a potential deal, most venture capital funds must make investments of at least $300,000 to $1 million. Typically, venture capitalists fund fewer than 1 percent of the deals that cross their desk. To give yourself the strongest shot at winning, ensure the credibility of your business plan by including additional verification from outside experts. Eliminate any obvious weak points. For example, if the chief executive or a key customer were to vanish suddenly, does the company have a back-up plan? If not, these financiers probably won't be interested.[2]

Remember that equity investors must be shown they can make significantly more money from an investment in your company than they can at current money market or CD rates. Otherwise, they'd be better off putting their money in those investments, which carry none of the risk.

Always show an appreciation for the equity capitalists' profit motive by including in your investment proposal a scenario demonstrating how they will be able to "cash out" within five years through a leveraged buyout by management, through a merger with a larger corporation, or by going public.

Venture capitalists are experienced businesspeople. In addition to obtaining their funding, you will also want to benefit from their business expertise by having them (and other outside experts they may recruit) sit on your board of directors.

Private Investment

If you have a small company and are trying to raise less than $300,000, try focusing on private investors as a source of capital. Private investors are usually wealthy individuals in your local area who have discretionary capital, people who want to be associated with a successful new enterprise. They are usually harder to find than venture capitalists; they don't advertise in the yellow pages. But the search is worth the effort, because they are more loyal and patient than venture capitalists. To find potential private investors, talk to your banker, attorney, CPA, professional business groups, and even state economic development organizations.

Private backers invest in your business for one primary reason: They expect to make a profit. So show them how they are going to make money by investing in your company.

Private investors generally don't require as detailed a business plan as a venture capital fund would. However, you still need a strong plan, with enough detail to show why and how you will succeed, one that demonstrates you have done an extensive analysis of your market. I recommend your plan be no more than fifteen to twenty double-spaced pages, plus supporting financials.

---

2. For detailed information on developing a business plan, refer to Chapters 4 and 6 of my book, *Beating the Odds: Ten Smart Steps to Small-Business Success* (New York: AMACOM, 1991).

In general, private investors are also experienced businesspeople. Therefore, you should also recruit them to serve on your board of directors.

As much as you want their money, be sure you are comfortable with your potential equity financiers, because you will be dealing with them for many years. So before you say yes, visit with bankers, CPAs, and executives of other companies they have invested in. After you've signed the papers, it's too late to change your mind.

Sacrificing Majority Ownership

As pointed out earlier, the more risk equity investors perceive, the more equity they will demand in return for their investment in your company. If your business has yet to turn a profit, equity investors may insist on majority ownership.

Entrepreneurs typically dread the thought of giving up majority ownership. If you are expanding and still unprofitable, you might waste all your energies trying to outfox your financiers just to ensure that you retain 51 percent of the company. And for what? Controlling interest provides no guarantee of genuine control; a disgruntled 5-percent shareholder can still cause you plenty of grief. Furthermore, your business may suffer in the process. You might even lose your company, as Ralph did.

Ralph is the pseudonym for a young businessman who came up to me after a speech I gave in Denver. Ralph complained that all venture capitalists were crooks. He had a super idea for a new company, involving a brand-new waste disposal technology.

Because of past debts, Ralph was unable to make any substantial investment in the business. However, he could demonstrate that the company would realize profits within ninety days of inception.

In spite of the fact that his written business plan was of poor quality, one venture capital firm offered to participate in exchange for 90 percent of the company's equity. Another firm offered him a $200,000 loan (secured by his equity), to be repaid as $1 million at the end of five years.

I told Ralph that in my opinion both offers were realistic, and I suggested that he seriously consider them. I also pointed out that, were he to choose the first offer, he could structure the deal to ensure that he would reacquire majority stock (subject to acceptable performance) after five years.

Ralph turned down both offers, and his gem of a company shriveled up and died. Ralph continues to curse equity investors to this day, without realizing that it was his reluctance to risk equity that caused the demise of his dream.

Unless your company currently shows a significant net worth or you can invest more cash in the deal, equity investors have every right to demand majority ownership in a young company as protection against their investment. No matter how much of a sure thing you believe you have, statistics show that the majority of early-stage businesses fail to make a profit—ever. In such an environment, investors are justified in asking for rewards commensurate with the risks.

The "Buy-Back" Clause

Just as your investors are justified in seeking to protect their interests, you are equally entitled to earn back controlling interest in your company over a specific period of time, subject to a specific sales/profits productivity formula. All you have to do is insert a buy-back clause into the investment agreement up front.

One way to structure a buy-back is to have a "call" in the agreement, requiring the outside investors to sell their shares to you at some multiple over a five-year period, subject to the company's performance. In this way, if you perform well, you can reacquire all of the company's stock.

Another option is to structure the agreement so that, over time (subject to performance and profitability), additional shares of stock will be issued to you at some multiple of the price paid by the investor, allowing you to regain majority ownership. In this scenario your payment for the additional shares will go to the company to provide additional operating capital.

Even if outside investors purchase majority stock ownership, try asking them to grant you the right to vote their controlling interest as long as you continue to meet or exceed your projections. In this case, the venture capitalists will own the stock, but as long as you perform to expectations, you will be given a proxy to vote their shares, allowing you to retain control over the operations of the company.

A final point: When you are about to find yourself a minority stockholder in your company, insist on a five-year employment contract with your equity investors (guaranteeing your executive position with the company unless you prove incompetent). This contract can also spell out yearly stock options for you (again, subject to performance). You may not have to ask for this contract; if investors believe your presence is essential to the company's success, they will insist on it.

Don't let your pride get in the way of a good deal. Just be creative in developing a buy-back agreement with your outside investor. Then be sure the investment agreement clearly spells out how you will regain majority ownership of the company. And in developing an agreement, always use an attorney experienced in business law and in dealing with companies similar to yours.

Remember, financiers don't want your company; they want your money. They want you to be a success—not because they like you, but because they want to make a profit on their investment. If you show them you are smart, understand your market, and can achieve the sales and profits you projected, they should be satisfied to let you run your company as you see fit. Remember to invite them to visit you frequently, so they can see for themselves how the business is doing.

How Much Cash Do You Think You Need? Double It!

When you develop your financial projections to determine how much funding your company needs, you make certain assumptions: Your products will be manufactured on time, your newly designed widget will work perfectly, customer orders will arrive each month as planned, the economy will stay healthy. If only half of your assumptions are realized, you will be lucky; nothing ever goes exactly according to plan. Furthermore, as hard as it is to raise money, it is usually easiest to raise the first time around. Therefore, whatever figure you initially project for your funding needs, *double this amount* to cover contingencies.

Does this mean that I'm telling you to raise $500,000 instead of $250,000? Absolutely. And I'm going to show you how to do it.

You believe you have an exciting company and that people are going to want to invest in it, right? *Then make them pay for the privilege.* Tell potential equity investors that your stock is being offered in ten blocks of $25,000; however, as part of the price of admission, for each block of stock, they will be expected to offer you a concurrent thirty-six-month loan for $25,000 at prevailing bank rates. In this manner, you can raise $250,000 as equity and an additional $250,000 as debt capital, giving you the buffer you need to cover contingencies.

Creative Equity Capital Sources

If you are asked to invest additional personal equity as the price for further outside equity investment and you find you are unable to do so, there are several creative options. If potential investors have faith in you and your company, they should be willing to help you structure creative collateral for the deal, while ensuring that their requirement for your increased investment is still met. Here are some options:

- Ask the equity investor to lend you the funds to use as your personal equity investment, with your company's stock, inventory, patents, and all product rights pledged to the investor as collateral for the loan. If your cash flow is going to be tight, try to structure the loan with no payments for the first twelve months.

- Instead of providing cash, offer a personal guarantee against the investor's note (with your home and/or other assets pledged as collateral).

- If you are confident of your sales projections, offer to provide a guarantee to the investor to the extent that retained earnings fall short of projections. (But remember—if sales fall short, you must pay the price.)

- Ask the investor to lend the required funds to the company, and offer the investor all other critical but thus far unencumbered assets of the company as security. You may think the assets are all tied up, but frequently some of the most valuable assets aren't (for example, the sole right to use the company's name, the exclusive rights to all patents, the exclusive rights to the customer list, full distribution rights for the product, and any improvements to the product). The pledge of these assets is accomplished at the time the new loan is entered into; the investor then contributes these assets to the company for its use. The investment agreement should also grant the executive the right to reacquire these assets for the same sum paid for them by the investor after the loan has been repaid.

- If you have confidence in your revenue projections, offer investors the maximum available equity in your company (up to 100 percent). Then insist on an option either to buy back the investors' shares (at a predetermined price and time) at some point in the future, subject to company performance, or to acquire additional company stock so that you can reacquire majority ownership (again at a predetermined price and time), with the funds going to the company, thus providing additional operating capital. (See the discussion under Sacrificing Majority Ownership earlier in this chapter.)

Other Capital Sources

State Government

Your state government probably offers financial assistance to early-stage companies, expanding businesses, and product development projects that bankers and equity capitalists won't touch.

However, don't make the mistake of believing your state has a pot of money you can dip into just for the asking. Access to these funds is subject to specific (and usually well-defined) rules. Usually these funds are available only if the financed activity will create a number of new jobs, so don't try to sell the glamour; sell the increased employment instead.

State economic development money is typically more difficult to secure than private financing, and it almost always comes with more strings. In this case, if it sounds too easy, it probably isn't.

When you do business within the halls of state government, be aware of the fact that the people you are dealing with are bureaucrats, not financiers. This means they usually won't take into account your future growth potential, the creativity of your product or service, or your management experience. Instead, they will consider how well you meet the requirements of their rulebook. This book may specify certain conditions, only some of which may be known to you. For example, they may consider how many new jobs will be created by a loan to your business, whether you have the strong written backing of your city, or whether your company is in one of your state's targeted growth industries. If you are considering applying for state funds, visit with your banker, with people who have been there before, and with local economic development groups so that you can uncover these hidden rules.

The cost of failing to follow the rules is high, as the following three stories demonstrate. These are tales that three entrepreneurs have shared with me about their frustrating experiences in dealing with state bureaucrats who "go by the rules":

- Terry, CEO of a flourishing manufacturing business, had been actively involved with his state's economic development commission for years. He knew all the key executives. He also knew some of the commission's hidden rules. For example, he knew that a business economic betterment loan should be applied for by the sponsoring city in which the business is located.

But when Terry decided to expand his business, he submitted his application directly to the commission's loan committee, since he knew several members of the committee and had worked with them over the years. He was turned down. Later, when he asked his city to resubmit the application, it was approved.

- Kerry had launched a new company and decided to approach her state's economic development office for financial support. The state offered a loan program that would fund the creation of new jobs. In fact, if Kerry's company created the required number of new jobs within a certain time period, the loan would be forgiven.

Kerry applied for the loan, but, because her business was expanding faster than anticipated, she began to hire the extra employees she needed before the loan was approved. When Kerry's loan came before the committee and the committee members learned that Kerry had already hired the new workers, her loan application was rejected. After all, they reasoned, she must not need their funds, since she had already created the new positions.

- Barry's struggling company had some past debts, but it also had an exciting product with a bright future. Barry sought a state product development loan to bring his new product to market. He was granted the loan; however, the loan agreement contained a clause specifying that the proceeds could be applied only to future costs associated with the new product.

Barry used a portion of the first installment of the loan to pay off old debts. As a result, he never saw the rest of the funds and is still struggling today.

Are any of these cases the state's fault? Hardly. Typically, impatient or poorly advised business executives plunge into the application process without understanding the rules of the game, believing that securing state money is far easier than conventional financing. This is a myth. If you plan to apply for state funding for your business, learn the rules—written and unwritten—and follow them.

Unconventional Cash Sources

When you've dipped into the conventional sources of capital and you still need to go back to the well, I can recommend some uncommon sources of capital, namely, people who understand your business and participate with you in some fashion (such as suppliers or customers). Following are some suggestions on how to attract their money:

- *Throw a vendor party.* If a number of your suppliers are located nearby, consider throwing either a "cost-cutting" or a "cash-raising" party. Rent a banquet room at a local hotel, and invite your vendors to a cocktail hour and dinner. After dinner, hand out material introducing some new products or services. Thank your vendors for their past support, discuss your new products, and follow up with a rousing marketing pitch on the projected growth of the company.

Finally, to help you achieve your stated goals (and depending on which type of party you decided to throw), ask your vendors for continued support, in the form of either suggestions for how they can help you reduce the cost of your inventory purchases or consideration of an equity investment in your company. If your vendors believe your growth projections, you'll probably have some takers.

- *Purchase manufacturers' equipment with equity.* If your company needs expensive machinery, consider offering equipment manufacturers equity in exchange for the equipment you need. If you can convince them your company has the potential for significant growth, they may jump at the opportunity. As shareholders, they will perceive you to be "locked in" to the use of their equipment as you expand. They may also offer you attractive discounts on subsequent orders.

- *Invite satisifed customers to become shareholders.* If you are blessed with satisfied customers who have discretionary capital, you may want to ask them for assistance. It is always easier to bring in new equity partners when they are enamored of your product or service. You have only to convince them that your sales and payback projections are realistic, and they should be willing to join forces with you.

- *Take advantage of area development programs.* In most states, there are two programs at your local and state level (both privately funded) that can supply loans for expansion and for acquisition of fixed assets. These are the 502 Local Development Company Program and the 504 Certified Development Company Program. Contact your Small Business Administration district office for further details.

If It Sounds Too Good to Be True . . . It Is!

Beware of the many business con artists out there. Always thoroughly check out the purveyors of incredible financing proposals. If a deal seems to good to be true, it probably is. If an organization promises you a "sure thing" for an up-front fee of several thousand dollars, walk away from it. Otherwise, the only sure thing is that they will have your money.

Managing Cash Flow

Whether you're still trying to complete the acquisition of your next round of capital or have already succeeded, there are some additional financial issues for you to consider—issues that can mean the difference between moderate success and stunning prosperity. These involve maintaining a healthy cash flow—the lifeblood of your company.

It is critical that you periodically analyze your company's cash situation. But many businesspeople, including successful ones, consider cash flow only when their auditors prepare year-end financial state-ments. If you don't follow your cash flow, plotting trends on a monthly basis, you may be missing the opportunity to maximize your company's performance. Furthermore, if you don't understand the flow of cash through your company, odds are your banker won't be interested in adding to it.

In its simplest form, a monthly cash flow statement is computed by taking the sum of all cash *uses* for the month and subtracting this amount from all cash *sources* for the same period. For some examples of how cash flow and income can differ significantly, take a look at Figure 6-2.

Some executives believe they need to worry about cash flow only if sales are poor. But severe cash flow problems may also be encountered by

Figure 6-2. Effects of various business events on cash flow.

Business Event	Cash Flow Statement	Income Statement	Balance Sheet
Sales of $150,000 this month, most of which is invoiced with 30 day terms but paid within 60 days.	Cash sources this month (comprising paid invoices from previous two months)* considerably less than reported sales.	Income statement sales greater than actual cash sources.	No significant cash flow impact.
Repayment this month of a $25,000 note to bank.	Cash uses for this month are greater (by $25,000) than expenses shown on income statement.	Not reflected on income statement (except possible slight reduction of interest payment).	No significant cash flow impact. Reduction in both assets (cash in bank) and liabilities (notes payable).
Depreciation of $300,000 worth of equipment on 60-month depreciation schedule ($5,000/month).	Monthly depreciation is not cash you spent; therefore, your monthly cash uses may be less than indicated on your income statement.	Monthly depreciation of $5,000 shows up on income statement as an expense.	No significant cash flow impact. Accumulated depreciation increase matched by fixed assets decrease.
Receipt of and payment for $100,000 in raw material/product inventory; but none yet utilized or sold.	Cash uses for the month are considerably greater (by this amount) than expenses shown on income statement.	Does not show up on income statement (until reflected as a cost of goods sold)	No significant cash flow impact. Increase in inventory and decrease in cash in bank.

* *A portion of your cash receipts for the current month consists of payment of invoices from previous month (thirty days) and from the month prior to that (sixty days); hence the statement "from the previous two months."*

businesses that are too successful—that is, those that are growing too fast. In this case, all the monthly income must be spent for additional inventory, leaving no cash to run the business. If a bank loan isn't planned for well in advance, management must either slow down the growth of the business (stretching out deliveries) or watch the business wither and die at the height of its success.

Your banker assumes you have the requisite experience to predict cash shortfalls well in advance. If you can't demonstrate the ability to project future cash flow deficits, your banker may not be interested in helping you during a panic cash shortfall. If an unforeseen cash crunch hits and you try to approach your banker at the last minute for additional cash to tide you over, your banker will probably refuse, and rightly so. After all, if you are such a poor manager that you overlooked your company's present cash hemorrhage, what else have you overlooked?

In general, it's a good idea to watch your cash flow monthly, plotting past results and projecting one or two years into the future. If your business is seasonal (e.g., a lawn care company in Alaska), a yearly cash flow statement will show you when to expect cash shortfalls, allowing you time to cover these contingencies with a short-term bank loan.

If you compute next year's cash flow projections and note a potential cash deficiency next summer, tell your banker *now*. If you present the image of an executive who is on top of things, your banker will probably agree to provide the cash you need next year.

Improving Cash Flow

There are a number of steps you can take to improve your company's cash flow. Let's review several options for increasing the inflow of cash and reducing cash outflows.

▪ *Increase your prices.* Believe it or not, the price for your product or service may be too low, sending a message to customers that the product or service is of low value as well. If you sell a big-ticket item and if you are priced in the low-to-middle range of the competition, consider positioning your product at the high end (on the basis of a better product, superior capabilities, or longer warranty) to generate additional cash.

▪ *Target your market niches.* It's better to cover a few markets with excellence than to blanket the world with mediocrity. Look at the size of the territory and the market niches you presently cover. Consider narrowing your primary market region to a one-day's drive from your office. Then define specific niche markets that are prime candidates for your product or service—hospitals and schools, for example—and go after these markets with a vengeance.

▪ *Sales calls—the more (and the more effective), the merrier.* If you find that it takes an average of ten calls to close a sale, focus on making more calls. You can increase sales even more by analyzing past sales calls to determine how many calls to a customer it takes, on average, to close a sale. If you find that, say, 80 percent of sales are closed on the first call to a customer, eliminate all second calls, and increase the number of one-time sales calls to prospective customers.

Finally, eliminate costly cold calls by initiating an introductory letter campaign to potential customers. Send out the letters, and then follow up with telephone calls for appointments.

▪ *Reduce receivables and increase payables.* Tell your best customers that you need some short-term help, and ask them to pay your invoices sooner; if you can reduce your receivables aging from sixty to thirty days, you gain an extra month's operating capital free of charge.

Also talk with your key suppliers, explaining that you need their help on a one-time basis. Ask to take forty-five days to pay their current invoices (but do this well before the due date). This will generate additional operating capital for your company.

▪ *Turn assets into cold cash.* Take a hard look at your company's assets. Sell those that are nonessential. Consider a sales-leaseback on the more expensive essential equipment that is relatively new. Contact any of the number of leasing companies participating in these programs, sell your assets to a leasing company for the cash you need, and then lease the equipment back.

Managing a Cash Crunch

Whether it's a seasonal shortfall or a severe economic downturn, if your company suddenly finds itself in a severe cash crunch, you can't sit around and wait. When the cash crisis is upon you, your suddenly solemn financiers will expect you to take decisive action to reduce expenses. You should focus on the following areas:

▪ *Reduce operating costs.* First, review all of your operations. If any products or services aren't contributing their fair share to profits, get rid of them. If certain product lines are growing by leaps and bounds, beware—this skyrocketing growth may be costing you plenty in terms of material and labor. By stretching out delivery times, you can scale back these costs as well and give revenues a chance to catch up.

If you can't analyze your expenses and sales by individual product line, you had better reorganize your accounting system fast. (Refer to the discussion of product-centered tracking in Step Five.)

If you are still doing all of your bookkeeping by hand, you are throwing money away. I recommend you get computerized fast. Depending on the size of your company, some accounting software programs (costing as little as a few hundred dollars) can do a good accounting job for your company while saving you far more than their cost each year.

Look at all your in-house activities to see if some of them (e.g., advertising, product assembly, telemarketing, computerized data management, or accounting) could be accomplished with less cost by utilizing outside firms.

Talk with your accountant and your attorney for some other ideas. For example, you may be able to utilize more junior personnel in their firms for more routine duties and thereby reduce their billings to you.

▪ *Initiate cutbacks and layoffs.* Next, you need to downsize your payroll costs appropriately. Review your staffing to identify absolutely essential positions. If it appears that layoffs will be necessary, first consider asking all your employees to work four days a week for a 20 percent cut in pay.

If this doesn't solve the cash problem, don't make the mistake of keeping people with nothing to do on the payroll just because you feel uneasy about laying them off. Unless you are willing to provide their paychecks out of your own savings, lay off your nonessential employees until you get over the hump. Execute your downsizing plan (as covered in Step Five) in a timely manner so you can get on with your survival tactics.

▪ *Curtail travel.* Aside from eliminating unnecessary travel, consider the following: If you are not already doing so, always ask for commercial and/or corporate rates when making hotel reservations. These are lower than regular rates, but lodging establishments won't offer them unless you ask. If occupancy rates are exceptionally low, as they may be during a recession, you can probably negotiate a rate that is even lower than the corporate rate.

If any of your traveling employees are fifty or over, offer to pay their $5 annual membership in the American Association of Retired Persons (AARP). They and you will reap additional travel discounts.

Many airlines offer fares that are up to 50 percent lower than regular fares if you stay over a Saturday night. When appropriate, encourage your employees to take advantage of these cheaper fares by offering to pay their weekend hotel costs.

If your employees are traveling near the end of the week, always check on weekend car rental rates, which are considerably lower than weekday rates. Many rental companies extend these rates Thursday through Sunday, but again you have to ask. Moreover, by joining certain low-cost associations indirectly affiliated with the government (like the Air Force Association), you can obtain near-government rates at certain major car rental companies and motels.

■ *Think frugal.* Whenever you authorize dollars to be spent, make sure they contribute directly to bottom-line profits. "Think Frugal" should be your slogan, even after your company's financial health starts to improve. Consider asking each employee to wear a "Think Frugal" button—this helps focus each individual to do his or her part in reducing the company's expenses.

As you undertake these cost-cutting steps, monitor your cash position daily in order to ensure that the hemorrhaging has stopped. Then draw up a six-month plan for securing new capital; you will need it even if your financial picture improves.

No company ever got hurt by constructive belt-tightening, but plenty have been slaughtered by trying to live high off the hog. If you use your scalpel wisely and fairly, you will have a leaner, meaner organization.

The sooner you act, the greater your company's chances for survival and the sooner you will see smiles again on the faces of your financiers.

EXERCISE: My Financial Perspective

After carefully reviewing this chapter, make a list of the financial problems and challenges your company faces. What are some creative steps you can take to address them?

---

* * *

You can be an astute financial manager, but if you don't have an aggressively, carefully developed marketing strategy, you are still throwing away profits. Enhancing your marketing effort is the focus of Step Seven of the Macrofruition process.

Step Seven

Expand Your Marketing Horizons

No matter how unique or exciting your product, without a strong marketing plan, you probably won't be able to raise the money you need to build your business and keep it growing. And even if you do raise the needed money, without a sound marketing effort, the lifetime of your exciting new product may be remarkably brief.

Without a dedicated marketing effort, your company is probably destined to limp along, rather than surge ahead. But even if your company is thriving, you may be throwing away additional profits unless you make a commitment to marketing excellence.

Step Seven of the Macrofruition process focuses on marketing your product to potential customers and on keeping those customers satisfied and coming back for more. I can't possibly cover in a single chapter all of the many marketing techniques available to you. So I'm going to focus on those elements of marketing that are typically overlooked or underutilized by busy executives—marketing factors that can strengthen your company's bottom line if you give them the attention they deserve.

Creating Your Annual Marketing Plan

Good marketing doesn't just happen; it is carefully planned. The first crucial step—and the one that is usually ignored by most companies—is the development of a sound marketing plan.

Your marketing plan defines how you intend to succeed with your

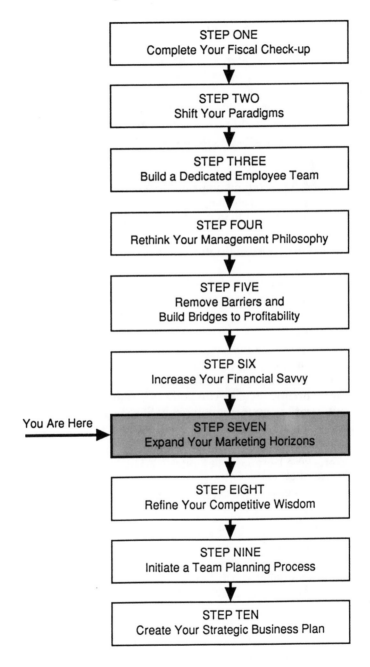

product or service in the marketplace. It is a part of your overall business plan.[1]

Start-up companies often develop marketing plans in order to secure funding. But the majority of established businesses don't have a written marketing plan. Most business executives don't realize that, in good times and bad, a thoroughly researched and well-executed marketing plan, updated yearly, could probably increase their sales significantly.

The primary purpose of your marketing plan is to help you understand three critical factors:

1. *Who* should be buying your product or service
2. *How* you should be selling to them
3. *Why* they will decide to purchase from you

Answer the Three Critical Questions: Who, How, and Why

All marketing plans must address the critical elements of *who, how,* and *why*. Without this knowledge, you can't hope to market your product effectively.

- *Who.* Start by identifying your major customers. You need to understand their spending patterns, as well as their needs and desires. You must also identify your competitors and how much potential customers are now spending on your competitors' products or services (we talk more about handling your competitors in Step Eight).

- *How.* How are you advertising your product or service to current and potential customers? What advertising medium are you using? What, and how effective, is your sales pitch? What is the best selling price strategy? Are you selling through retail outlets, direct salespeople, telemarketing, or direct mail? Which avenues are the most effective, and why?

- *Why.* Potential customers won't purchase your product simply because it's innovative or because it will save them money. People have a natural resistance to buying *anything*. So, in trying to attract new business, you must answer the question "What does this product do for customers?"

---

1. Your business plan (of which your marketing plan represents but one section) also includes sections on your management team, manufacturing, operations, administration, and finance.

I learned this lesson from a painful experience in the early 1970s. I was so proud of the first flyer I had created for my MinAlert™ monitoring console. The product had terrific features, including a self-testing capability and a lifetime guarantee. I emphasized all of these impressive features in my flyer, and I was elated with the beautiful layout.

I took the new flyers to my first trade show, spread them out on a table, and anxiously waited. Potential buyers stopped, picked up the flyer, studied it, studied it, and studied it some more. Then they set it back down and moved on.

I failed with that flyer because I failed to answer the most important question in the minds of my would-be customers: "*Why* should I purchase this product?" They didn't want to build my product; they didn't even want to understand how it worked. They wanted to know why they should buy it, and I had failed to give them a reason.

Think of every potential buyer as wearing a giant sign. Each sign reads, "What Will Your Product Do For Me?" If you answer this question, you may have a new customer. If you don't answer this question, you haven't got a chance.

EXERCISE: My Initial Marketing Plan Homework

Open your notebook and write three brief paragraphs that address each of the three categories above—who, how, and why—as the first step in developing your written marketing plan. Note the order: You need to identify *who* your customers are before you can determine *how* to market to them and *why* they will choose your product or service.

Develop Growth Projections

The next step in developing your marketing plan is to determine your market share and to develop growth projections.

If you are entering a new market, you can use the following method to size your market and to predict annual sales. You can also use it to measure your progress (and current share) in existing markets. If you have an established, ongoing company, a realistic growth goal might be 10 percent per year.

First, determine the scope of your marketplace or sales territory. Is it your city, your county, your state, your region of the country, or the entire United States? (Let's assume you determine your territory is your county.)

Next, analyze the typical buyers, or target customers, for your product or service. (Assume you determine your target customers to be women between eighteen and thirty years of age.)

Then, determine how many target customers there are in the sales territory you defined. (We'll assume there are 200,000 women between eighteen to thirty in your county.)

From these data, you can predict how many buyers will purchase your product or service for the next several years. A conservative estimate in a new market might be 0.5 percent of the total market in the first year, 1.0 percent in the second year, and 1.5 percent in the third year. (In our example: 0.5 percent of 200,000 equals 1,000 unit sales the first year—assuming each woman buys only one unit—so total projected sales would be 1,000 multiplied by the unit price.)

EXERCISE: Sizing Your Market and Your Sales

Using the above procedure, estimate the size of your current and potential markets, and calculate potential sales of your product or service to those markets for the next five years.

Write the Actual Plan

After you have determined the size of your market and your potential share of it for the next five years, begin to write the actual plan, starting with the *introduction*. First, describe your company's strengths and weaknesses and those of your competition. Then, describe how you identify, contact, and sell to existing customers and how you plan to attract potential customers and sell to them. Detail how you set your price and what type of sales force you use. Finally, include a summary of why you are succeeding and will continue to succeed.

The next section of the marketing plan describes your *objectives*. Here you outline the broad marketing goals you are trying to achieve and tie them to a specific time frame (e.g., twenty-five new accounts next year or $500,000 in sales by year-end).

After this section comes the *strategies* section, in which you present a detailed description of the programs you will undertake (e.g., a regional advertising campaign, the appointment and training of eight new sales representatives) to achieve your objectives.

In the last section of the marketing plan, list your *tactics*—the detailed actions required to implement your strategies (e.g., the new ads you are developing, the magazines in which you'll advertise, the lead tracking system you are using, the creation of new product literature).

When you have completed this exercise, you will have a solid written plan that you can use to attack your market and to win customers away from the competition.[2]

Effective Advertising

No matter how good a product or service is, unless you prime the pump with *sustained* advertising, the well of orders usually dries up. Most potential customers do not decide to buy a new product because they see it in a single ad or news release. They act only after seeing several additional ads for the product, which reinforce their need for the product and confirm the company's viability.

To resolve where and how you will advertise (newspapers, magazines, radio, or TV), decide which medium reaches your audience most effectively. For example, if you provide a specialized product to automotive buffs throughout the country, a magazine like *Car and Driver* is a perfect advertising medium. If you provide a service to all homeowners in your local area, local newspapers might be a good choice.

Budget your advertising dollars for an ongoing campaign, trying to hit the public with multiple ads spread out over a period of time. Be sure that your ads have a strong call to action, telling potential customers what they should do next.

Then sit back and start taking orders. Whenever possible, try to ascertain where the orders originated, so you'll know how effective your advertising was. If you have a mail-order business and run ads in several magazines or newspapers, include different fictitious department numbers in your mailing address so that you will know which ad generated the most orders.

Make sure your product's selling price allows you to recoup the cost of advertising. If a $500 ad generates fifty sales, you should build a $10 advertising expense into the cost of each product to ensure that you always have advertising funds available for the next marketing campaign. (If your price is then no longer competitive, this should serve as a red flag to warn you that your advertising costs may be too high.)

2. For a more detailed discussion of how to develop a marketing plan, refer to Chapter 3 of my book, *Beating the Odds: Ten Smart Steps to Small-Business Success* (New York: AMACOM, 1991).

Secrets of Successful Print Advertising

If your ads and brochures look cheap, stress product features, or have no "call to action," they may be failing to attract the customers you seek. Because young businesses are often strapped for dollars, their executives tend to cut corners on print advertising and on other printed materials. In many cases, however, these materials may be the only part of your company the buyer sees. If they look cheap, the buyer will assume that your company and your product are cheap. If you give your ads a high-quality look, you'll be perceived as having a high-quality product.

This doesn't mean you necessarily need an expensive, full-color brochure. But you should at least print your brochures and other print ads in two colors on good-quality, glossy stock. And don't have your cousin take the photographs; leave that job to a professional photographer.

When it comes to getting the words right, your best bet is to have a professional write the text. If you spend the money for this effort, make sure your copywriter asks a lot of questions first in order to understand fully your product. If you simply can't afford this option now, then choose the best writer in the company to compose the text.

Finally, your ads should always have a strong "call to action." Here are some suggestions: Have a mail-in coupon as part of the ad, or offer a toll-free phone number for more information (with the fierce competition in the telecommunications industry, the cost of "800" phone numbers is surprisingly inexpensive), or offer a free gift if customers bring the ad to your store. Whatever device you choose, just be sure you motivate customers to take action *now*.

Beware of Your Image

If your company does business by mail, take a good look at your company literature, your business cards, and your stationery. If they look cheap, then no matter how hard you try, your company and your products will be perceived as cheap. So strive to give your company's literature the look of success.

Beware of newspaper ads offering 500 business cards for a pittance. Don't skimp here; a cheap business card says you have a cheap business.

I recommend using an artist or even a college art class doing a class project to design your logo or stationery. Then have the logo printed on quality paper (business stationery is printed on twenty-pound stock, so consider twenty-four-pound stock to set your company apart).

Never use just a post office box for an address. This gives your business the image of a boiler-room operation—here today, gone tomorrow. Avoid this image by including your street address or by using a private mailbox, listing the address of the service and your "suite number" (which is really your mailbox number).

Finally, if you meet customers in person, always remember that the way you dress contributes to a customer's image of your company. If you look successful, you strengthen the image of your successful company.

How to Generate (Almost) Free Publicity

An effective and inexpensive way to expand your advertising effort is to become a recognized expert in your field. For example, if you own a travel agency, you could distribute frequent news releases to the media on some aspect of business travel. You might also consider writing free-lance articles for area publications. If your name is known, chances are that when a big travel story breaks—say, a major airfare increase for business travelers—you will be interviewed by your local TV stations as an authority on the subject. Your agency's name will appear in the interview, once again reminding the world that you (and your company) are experts in business travel. The result? More business.

Tricks of the Trade Show

Studies consistently show that trade shows are the least expensive method of generating potential new leads.[3] This assumes, of course, that you participate in the trade shows that are most likely to be attended by your potential customers and that therefore will generate the most business for your company.

To get the most bang for the buck, try for a corner booth, even if it costs a little more. People always slow down at the crossroads, so there is a better chance they will see what you have to offer. And a corner booth gives you the added benefit of exposure on two different aisles.

Be forewarned that there may be hidden set-up costs in a few locations. If you participate in a show in New York, Chicago, or Los Angeles, the strong trade unions will have you in their grip. You'll have to hire the teamsters to carry your exhibit into the hall, even if your display is small. You'll have to hire the carpenters' union to set up your booth,

---

3. In 1988, the McGraw-Hill Laboratory of Advertising Performance reported that the average cost to close a sale by calling on customers was almost 3.5 times greater than the cost to close a trade show lead.

and you'll have to hire the electrical union to plug in your display. Don't try to bypass the unions in these cities, or they will shut your booth down. However, in most other cities, union labor is usually an option, rather than a requirement.

Aside from having an attractive booth, a constant presence is essential. Never leave your booth empty, no matter what the reason; an empty booth tells the potential customers you really don't care. I recommend having a minimum of two people work the show so that your booth will still be occupied when one of you takes a break. And don't eat in your booth; keep it neat and businesslike.

Sitting down in a chair is another no-no. People walk by, see you sitting, and immediately perceive you as being lazy. Or they become angry because their feet hurt and yours don't. Either way, you lose.

Yet standing for a full day's show is really tough, so here is a tip: At the front of your booth, place a covered table that is forty-two inches high, instead of the usual thirty-six inches. Then place bar stools behind it. Now you can take a load off your feet while you still appear to be standing.

Always have some literature to hand out: product/service brochures, show specials, your business card. Then, if other people stop at your exhibit while you are busy with a prospect, they can still pick up something to remember you by. Try to distribute as much literature as possible, and make sure all literature has your company name, address, and phone number on it. Also consider a giveaway, making sure that the prizes are valuable. Have sign-up cards and a stuff box available. Ask for name, address, and phone number on the form. Include a check-box for customers to indicate whether they would like more information or a free estimate of your product or service. These entry forms then become sales leads.

Always strive to present the best possible company image at a trade show. The image you present will determine whether people stop and talk to you (or even call you later).

Make sure you dress for the successful look, even if you aren't. People like to associate with success, but dressing down to be informal or "folksy" tells customers that you haven't made it yet.

Maintain eye contact with passers-by, and always greet them with a smile: "Hi there. Can I offer you some free information on our new lawn widget?" Practice your pitch before the show so that you will know the answers and will sound both professional and at ease when you answer questions.

Visit your competitors openly. Take their literature, ask them questions, and invite them to your booth. You don't want to reveal any trade secrets, but you want them to reveal as much as possible about what they're doing.

Remember that your purpose in attending the trade show is to generate business leads. Prepare a series of small forms, which you can conceal in your coat pocket, that include the following categories: customer name, product interest or application, customer's specific need, what the customer is trying to achieve (i.e., the problem the customer wants to solve), the customer's decision time frame, the decision process, name of the decision maker, how the customer wants to proceed.

Leave space to answer each question on the form. After visiting with a prospect, fill out the form immediately (this should take only a minute or so). Finally, prioritize the lead as A (Hot, or ready to purchase now); B (Warm, or high interest but future decision); or C (Cool, or a tire-kicker who is just looking).

Later, you can sort the leads and follow up with the As first and the Bs next. Don't bother to do much more with the Cs than send literature and follow up six months later.

Surviving the Competitive Bidding Process

Many companies pursue some portion of their business in the form of competitive bidding. This is a specialized marketing game that requires detailed knowledge in order to win. Unless you know you will always be the low bidder and thereby win every job you bid, I strongly suggest you develop a specific marketing checklist to evaluate potential bid opportunities.

Unless your win rate is better than 75 percent, you are probably bidding a number of jobs that you should not be wasting your resources on. Analyze those bids you lose to see if a consistent pattern is emerging. If this analysis reveals a specific weakness, fix it. You can use the marketing checklist in Figure 7-1 to help you evaluate the pros and cons of entering into competitive bidding on a particular contract.

Marketing to Uncle Sam

As your business grows, you will continue to seek lucrative new markets for your products or services. Such prospecting leads many business executives to consider selling to the federal government. There are several critical marketing aspects to consider.

Figure 7-1. Competitive project/program checklist.

IS THE CUSTOMER COMMITTED TO THIS PROJECT/PROGRAM?
(as opposed to it's being a manager's "nice-to-have" idea)

■ What generated the need for this project/program: a technology breakthrough, demands from customers significant changes in the marketplace, a strong price advantage, or something else?

■ What is the customer's timing and priority for this project/program? What other options does the customer have in addition to pursuing this project/program?

■ Does the customer's senior management endorse the project/program?

■ How does the customer plan to procure the products or service (is the customer willing to pay for development or is it looking for an off-the-shelf product? What will the project/program require from us (a new product, new manufacturing equipment, additional service staff)?

■ What is the customer's budget for this project/program?

CAN WE WIN THIS PROJECT/PROGRAM?

■ What are the real advantages of our concepts/products/capabilities? Do we have provable benefits? Will our proposed solution be cost-effective?

■ Do we have product/service ideas or innovations that provide the customer with clear, measurable, low-risk advantages?

■ Do we have direct applicable experience and an excellent track record with this customer? If not, do we have an admirable track record with similar customers?

■ Is our best group of employees available to tackle the proposal? Can we provide this team the resources needed to generate a winning proposal?

■ Are we committed to winning the bid, and do we have a believable approach to managing applicable project/program risks?

■ What are our competitors' probable approaches? Their strengths and weaknesses? How will their proposed solutions stack up against ours?

■ How hungry are our competitors (how aggressive will they be on pricing?), and how hard will they compete to win this program?

■ Have our competitors been working this program with the customer far longer than we have? If so, how can we mitigate any advantage they might have gained? Could they have influenced the procurement to favor their product?

■ Can we develop a cost-effective approach that will be responsive to all the customer's requirements? At a price that will win?

■ How will we demonstrate a clear understanding of the customer's requirements for this project/program? Can we identify the key problem areas, as well as our potential solutions to these problems?

■ How can we convince the customer we have a low-risk approach to solve these problems? What experimentation, research, or other technical efforts should we undertake to provide the customer with a convincing argument?

■ Can we influence the customer's plans and budgets? Do we need to convince the customer's top executives that we offer the best solution? If so, how? Do we need to run tests or demonstrations as part of this persuasion effort?

■ Are there political, economic, or environmental ramifications to consider?

IS THIS PROJECT/PROGRAM WORTH IT?

- What is this project/program's business potential for our company, in terms of orders, sales, profits, and ROI (return on investment)? What resources are required and what does our spending curve look like?

- Will the required resources have an impact on other programs? How strategically important is this opportunity relative to the planned growth we envision for our business?

- If we decide not to pursue this opportunity, what are the consequences of this decision to us, to our competitors, and to our customer?

TO SUM UP OUR COMMITMENT TO THIS PROJECT/PROGRAM:

- Are we willing to dedicate the maximum effort required to win and implement this project/program?

- Do we have the best solution and the best team assigned to this effort?

- Will we have a winning approach, a competitive price and a proposal that will make us money?

The Pitfalls of Federal Government Projects

Government purchasing organizations aren't run by businesspeople, they're run by bureaucrats who base their decisions, not on sound business sense, but on the lowest risk to their careers.

When Uncle Sam assembles an RFP (Request for Proposal) to develop and build a screwdriver, project bureaucrats start adding a lot of lengthy "boilerplate" requirements (originally developed during past programs) to the document. The RFP may swell to several hundred pages, calling out traceability back to the suppliers of the metal for the blade and the plastic for the handle, as well as requiring periodic laboratory stress tests on the product and government inspectors on your assembly line. This also means that the government can audit your books at any time and that the bureaucrats can shut you down if they find something they don't like. Finally, even if you do have the lowest price, you may lose the order because you're not in a certain congressional district. All of this adds to your cost of proposing and selling to the government and to the final price of the screwdriver.

Here's a real-life example from my own experience of how the costs of doing business with the government can spiral. When I worked for a company in the aircraft industry, our raw material cost to purchase a sophisticated display screen for a commercial aircraft was $4,000. But our cost to purchase the *identical size component* for a military aircraft (which means it had to meet the aforementioned boilerplate requirements, go through government testing, and so on) was $30,000!

I belabor this point so that you will be aware, when bidding on government projects, of how your costs of meeting government requirements can escalate beyond all reasonable estimates. Novice bidders can find themselves on the verge of bankruptcy if they don't understand the rules of the game.

In addition to being cognizant of the costs involved, you must be aware of the other, inevitable frustrations of dealing with government bureaucracy, especially with the military. Military program offices are usually managed by career military officers who may occupy the program management position for only a few years before being assigned to another post. It is not uncommon to spend one or two years working with a specific government program team and then, in the middle of the program, suddenly find that the program staff is being replaced by a completely new team, none of whom understands the program or your widget and all of whom will now judge you only on the written letter of the signed contract.

The Bidding Process

When seeking competitive bids, the government issues either (1) an RFQ (Request for Quote) for price quotes for an item already in government inventory, or (2) an RFP (Request for Proposal) for proposals to develop, qualify, and manufacture a new item not in inventory. (As I present a representative flow for the bidding process, keep in mind that your bid activities may vary slightly from this norm.)

Certain RFPs are designated as small-business set-asides, which means they are reserved for small businesses employing fewer than 500 people.[4] If your company falls into this range, you will improve your odds of winning by focusing your efforts on these projects.

RFPs come in a variety of flavors; three of the most common are:

1. *FFP* (Firm Fixed Price), in which you will receive exactly the price you propose
2. *CPFF* (Cost Plus Fixed Fee), in which you will receive your actual cost plus an additional 10 to 15 percent
3. *CPIF* (Cost Plus Incentive Fee), in which you will receive your cost

4. If your business employs more than 500 people, is engaged in manufacturing, and is not dominant in your industry, it may still be eligible for a small-business designation. Contact your nearest SBA (Small Business Administration) office for further clarification.

plus an additional 10 to 15 percent, provided you meet certain specified contract incentives

The RFP (or RFQ) usually references a number of FARs (Federal Acquisition Regulations), as well as a number of government specifications. Don't panic, but also don't take anything for granted. Contact the contracting officer, and ask for copies of any referenced documents.

New government programs are always announced in the Commerce Business Daily (CBD). This publication is available by subscription[5] and is carried by many larger libraries. It is also available through on-line computer databases.

However, don't wait until a program appears in the CBD to decide to pursue it. Chances are that your competition has been courting the program managers for many months prior to the CBD notice, helping with the specifications and suggesting certain program changes. It probably has a good idea what the customer is expecting in terms of a winning price. Therefore, you had better learn to cultivate contacts yourself if you hope to win at this game.

If you haven't visited with the program personnel before the RFP hits the street, it's too late. When the RFP is sent out to prospective bidders, the door slams shut and the government program personnel can no longer talk with you. All future interaction must be with the contracting officer, who usually knows nothing except when your quote is due.

So if you are going to bid government programs, start early and get to know both the players and the program. If there are some unnecessary specifications or irrelevant boilerplate requirements, explain to the key program staff why these elements should be relaxed or eliminated from the RFP.

I recommend using the marketing checklist presented in Figure 7-1 as a way of ensuring that you have all the information you need. In addition, for government programs, you should include some additional elements on your checklist; these are detailed in Figure 7-2.

After your quote is submitted, you may be notified that you made the "short list." This is the first cut, eliminating those proposals deemed "noncompliant" or too far outside the price window to be considered seriously.

At this point, a list of questions may be sent to you for your response,

5. Contact the Superintendent of Documents, Government Printing Office, Washington, D.C. 20402-9373 (telephone: 202-783-3238). The cost is approximately $270 per year with first-class mailing, and checks, Visa, and MasterCard are accepted.

Figure 7-2. Additional items for military competitive checklist.

- Are the funding organization, the procuring (contracting) organization, and the user organization (which are probably all in different locations) and Congress all solid supporters of the program?

- Are there new military threats or other problems* that have generated this requirement?

- Has our company established significant contact with the customer before the program was budgeted? Before the program appeared in the CBD?

- What is the program's proiority within the Department of Defense? What is the DoD's acquisition plan (e.g., is the DoD ready to pay for a new product or willing only to accept an off-the-shelf product)?

- Have we worked—either by ourselves or with the DoD—to analyze the threat that necessitated this procurement, to help create the specifications for the product, and/or to prove our proposed product's value in solving the problem that necessitated the DoD's requirement for this program?

- Have we helped the program office to configure the program and its preferred solution into a product we can offer?

---

*Suppose you were focused on a specific agency, such as the FAA. Typical examples of these "other problems" might include a lack of security at U.S. airports or commercial aircraft overcrowding in U.S. airspace. These problems usually receive considerable media coverage.

and additional specification changes may be made by the government, after which you may be asked to resubmit your bid. Or you may be asked for a Best And Final Offer (BAFO); in this case, the government gives you a last chance to modify (translation: lower) your bid.

Finally, you are notified whether you've won the bid, after which the government may decide unilaterally to change the project specifications again. But don't complain too loudly, or the bureaucrats may reopen the competitive bidding process. Or the contract may be subsequently canceled because Congress didn't continue to fund subsequent phases of the program.

With a fiendish process like this, it's a wonder that any company bothers to bid for government projects. However, the lure of sizeable, ongoing orders draws many companies into the fray.

Why Proposals Lose

In all of my dealings with the government, thanks to my use of the checklists in Figure 7-1 and Figure 7-2, I have compiled a record of winning more than 90 percent of the contracts I went after. I also have compiled a list of the most common reasons bids are rejected:

- *Chasing programs with no authorized funding.* If there is no funding available, an RFP will never be issued, no matter how much the program staff may want it. If an agency talks to you about a program, find out if the program is real before you waste a lot of time and energy, only to find out it was just a pipe dream. Talk to your legislators and other government sources to see if funds have been allocated (it is illegal to issue an RFP or RFQ without funds, so once the request is issued, you know funding exists—but do you know how much?).

- *Waiting to work the program actively until you receive the RFP.* If you wait until this moment to start your pursuit, you are far behind most of the competition, which already knows most of the unwritten requirements as a result of past dialogue with the customer.

- *Failure to consider the political factors that may affect the award.* Does one political party want the program, whereas the other side of the aisle is pushing a different agenda? Are legislators in your congressional district considered promilitary? Are they active and influential with military budgets and authorizations?

- *Believing the government can always afford your price.* The government is not a bottomless pit of money. Try to learn from other organizations and from funding profiles what the probable funding is for your program, and then make an offer that the government can afford.

- *Adding extra "bells and whistles" to your proposed product.* There is no real value in offering more than the specifications require. Be careful, because you may be making your proposal more attractive at the expense of a higher price. Your proposal will be evaluated only on the basis of the RFP requirements, not on your extras.

- *Underestimating your true costs.* Determine what the government will expect from you in terms of compliance and reporting paperwork if you win. The cost of these requirements may be prohibitive; in any event, you had better build the cost of this compliance into your proposal. If the cost of your proposal is too low, the government may disqualify you for obvious pricing oversights.

- *Failure to respond to all items requested.* When preparing a bid, go to Section B of the RFP to learn exactly what items and services the customer wants.[6] Then make sure your proposal is responsive to all these issues so that you won't be judged "noncompliant" and be thrown out.

- *Submitting your proposal late.* Allow plenty of time. You may ask for an extension when you first receive the RFP (which you may or may not be granted), but don't expect an extension at the last minute. No matter how good your proposal is, if it is one minute late (even if it's not your fault), it won't be considered.

- *Failure to understand the customer's Most Important Requirements (MIRs).* These may not be obvious in the RFP, but, if you have been working with the customer in advance, you should have a good idea what they are (and price isn't always one of them). Once you know these requirements, you need to develop a winning strategy to satisfy the majority of these requirements better than any other competitor.

- *Failure to work with the real decision makers.* Make sure you are dealing with the true decision makers, not just worker bees on an ego trip.

Not all government projects are as complicated or fraught with potential problems as I may have implied, but you must be careful when you enter this market. If you are truly serious about pursuing government business, I strongly recommend you consider taking one of a number of government acquisition seminars that are offered throughout the country. Contact your legislators and the Economic Development Office of the Department of Commerce in Washington, D.C., your state economic development office, or your nearest Small Business Development Center or Small Business Administration district office for additional details. Government-sponsored seminars are good, but my experience has been that the private seminars are better, especially if they are run by personnel who have had extensive experience dealing with the government acquisition system.

---

6. The sections accompanying a typical RFP are as follows: Section A: the Solicitation/Contract Form; Section B: Supplies or Services and Prices/Costs; Section C: the Description, Specification, and Work Statement; Section D: Packaging and Marking Requirements; Section E: Inspection and Acceptance Procedures; Section F: Required Deliveries or Performance; Section G: Contract Administration Data; Section H: Special Contract Requirements; Section I: Contract Clauses; Section J: List of Attachments; Section K: Representations, Certifications, and Statements; Section L: Instructions, Conditions, and Notices; Section M: Evaluation Factors for Award.

The World Is Your Oyster: International Marketing

If you are considering expanding into overseas markets, there are some elements of international marketing you should contemplate. In the space of a few pages, I can't make you a foreign affairs expert, but I can help you develop an awareness of what lies ahead with your international dealings, as well as cover some basic do's and don'ts.

When you decide to approach foreign markets, many of the rules change. Unfortunately, no one tells you what the new rules are; it's your job to research them before you approach your new market.

Every country has its own ways of doing business. If you adapt to the ways of each country, you may win new business, but if you try to force your ways upon international customers, you are destined to lose.

An effective secret in gaining an advantage in specific foreign countries is to develop key contacts in those countries. You need a friend or ally in the country, whether an agent, a dealership, a consultant, or a trading company. In some cases, companies within a particular country will undertake joint ventures with you, and they may even provide capital for your business.

How do you find these vital liaisons? Start by meeting people in your own city or region of the country who are natives of the countries in which you want to expand. Ask them about the rules of doing business in their country, and ask them to recommend possible business contacts.

Contact the target country's nearest attache or embassy. Contact your legislators in Washington to arrange introductions at the embassy. Make an appointment with the business affairs officer or the appropriate business development official. Explain to that person exactly what your business is, specifically what you want to do in his or her country, and what type of assistance you are seeking.

Many state governments sponsor trade missions to foreign countries to promote business contacts. Contact your state legislators or state economic development office for more information.

Investigate export regulations (tariffs, duties) for your products. Your congressional delegation in Washington should be able to help you with this task.

Items always sell for more overseas, because of the additional costs of doing business in a foreign country, such as maintaining a rep there. Compare your anticipated international selling price with the price of similar products in the country of interest to make sure your product will be competitive.

Study the market and the customs in the foreign country of interest.

Here are three keys to success:

1. Form strategic business alliances within the country.
2. Know the key elements of the marketplace in that country.
3. Complete a competitive assessment so that you know who your foreign competitors are, how their goods are priced, and how you will secure a portion of their market share.

You should also be concerned with the manner in which you will be paid. Exchange rates can fluctuate as much as 25 percent in the space of a few months. You need to forge an arrangement that shares this risk with your foreign partners.

When putting written agreements together, you must consider whose country's laws will apply. Have your lawyer visit with your customer's attorney to work out the details.

Form an opinion as to the future needs of the target country's marketplace. This will help you to determine products to develop for the market. Don't just offer the stateside versions of your product. If these people have unique needs, offer what they want.

In each country, always know some key phrases and greetings in the local language. If you have an employee who is from the country or who speaks the language—whether a senior manager or a clerk—take him or her along to assist you.

Beware of the perceived image of the ugly American (translated: pushy, arrogant, discourteous, noisy, and conceited). Go out of your way to counteract this perception by trying to fit in with the local culture.

I strongly recommend that, if you intend to work with a specific country, you contact your library for books on customs within that country.

I have found the following general reference books to be of invaluable assistance:

- All of Roger Axtell's international reference books, in particular, *Do's and Taboos Around the World: A Guide to International Behavior*, 2d ed. (New York: Wiley, 1990); *Do's and Taboos of Hosting International Visitors* (New York: Wiley, 1990)(great for when they visit you); and *Do's and Taboos of International Trade: A Small Business Primer* (New York: Wiley, 1989).

- *Pan Am's World Guide: The Encyclopedia of Travel* (New York: McGraw-Hill, 1982). Pan Am may be gone, but the 26th edition is still in print and is a great reference because most of the information is still applicable; I hope McGraw-Hill will consider updating it soon.

Whatever country you set your sights on, if you study up on the customs of that country, you will put your prospective business partners at ease—the first step on the road to a successful relationship with offshore businesses.

Customer Service: Your Secret Marketing Weapon

Several years ago, my city had two discount electronics stores, one called Best Buy and the other called King. Both offered similar products at competitive prices. Their locations and facilities were comparable.

At Best Buy, customers were always greeted with a smile. The salespeople were there to help you or to leave you alone, depending on what you wanted. The store maintained an in-house service department.

At King, the sales people were indifferent—when you could find them. And since there was no service department, the store had to ship merchandise away when service was required.

Not surprisingly, the King store closed its doors. Best Buy, on the other hand, continues to prosper. The difference between the two stores can be summed up in a single word: service.

Have you ever asked yourself why some businesses with mediocre products become successful, while other companies with brilliant products fail? Chances are that a strong element of customer service was part of the success equation, whereas a lack of service contributed to the business failures.

The Customer *IS* the Business

From a business perspective, customers are our only reason for existing. Think about that statement for a moment. Bankers provide capital so that we can secure the materials we need to meet the demands of our customers. We provide paychecks so that our employees can support their families while they build, sell, and deliver our goods to customers. But only our customers, by purchasing what we have to offer, provide profits for our business. So you had best treat your customers well. Sure, there are times when deadlines and problems can add up to a pressure-cooker environment, but that's why you are sitting in the senior executive's chair. Don't use the pressures of the job as an excuse to ignore or neglect the people who are responsible for keeping you in business.

Keeping your customers satisfied ensures that your company will build a strong legacy of repeat orders. Other activities can afford to be delayed; there is nothing more important than serving your customers well.

Building Customer Loyalty

If you make sales only to customers who never come back, you constantly have the expense of attracting new one-time customers. But if you retain those first-time customers through exceptional customer service, they come back for more, and you have an ongoing annuity.

It may take a long time to win a new customer, but you can lose one in a few seconds. And you may never know it, because if you wait for your customers to call with a problem, you may have already lost them.

So how do you keep customers? By giving them what they want, fixing problems fast, and letting them know you care. If you have a product, do you have an upgrade program that allows for add-ons later? Or a periodic service program to keep their widget in tip-top shape? If you have a service business, can you offer additional options to satisfied customers?

How many times have you contacted your customers after the sale to be sure they were satisfied? A strong follow-up program means fixing any problems fast and to the customer's satisfaction.

The relationship you have with your customer or client doesn't end with the sale unless you want it to. And if you do end it there, you won't ever have a growing business. If you have a strong customer follow-up program and your competitors don't, you will win the marketing game. But if they do and you don't, you'll lose.

Fixing Customer Problems

Not long ago, I remember seeing a sign in a friend's office that stated two rules for dealing with customers:

Rule #1—The customer is always right.
Rule #2—If you believe the customer is ever wrong, refer
　　　to Rule #1.

It costs you time and money to win a new customer. If your customer makes a purchase from you and then has a problem, you have a problem. If you choose to ignore it, it may go away, but so will the customer.

Let me share with you a refreshing perspective I learned from the authors of a top-notch book on customer service, *Delivering Knock Your*

Socks Off Service.[7] When your customer has a problem, you shouldn't focus just on fixing the problem; what you really want to do is fix the *customer*.

To do this, start by listening to what your customer is saying. Let the person vent his or her frustrations, and pay close attention to what is being said. Then respond by telling the customer you are sorry about the problem.

Put yourself in your customers' shoes. If the problems would frustrate you as a customer, say so, and the customer will believe you are on his or her side.

After you have discussed the problem and you have come up with some ideas on how to remedy it, suggest a solution—or several possible solutions—to the customer, such as sending someone out to correct the problem, shipping a new unit, or having the customer return the broken item for adjustment. Then ask the customer what he or she would like you to do; involve the customer in the solution process.

If your suggestions are met with an indifferent response, you haven't solved the real problem. Keep probing, and ask the customer for suggestions. You might consider offering a rebate, a discount, or a free gift for the customer's trouble. When you and the customer agree on what needs to be done, do it and do it promptly, so that both the problem and the customer are fixed.

Finally, follow up with a call or letter to the customer to ensure that all is well once again. This kind of response is also a super advertisement, because the newly satisfied customer will spread the word to potential customers about your incredible response.

Every time you deal with a customer's problem, make the process a learning experience for you. The customer has probably done you a favor by uncovering a weak point in your system. So after you have cured the customer's problem, make sure you take strong corrective action so that the problem never occurs again.

Turning Swords Into Plowshares

No matter how hard you strive to deliver exemplary service, you are bound to come across an irate customer from time to time.

Have you ever been faced with a customer who was angered by a delivery problem over which you had no control? Here is an example of

---

7. Kristin Anderson and Ron Zemke, *Delivering Knock Your Socks Off Service* (New York: AMACOM [paperback], 1991).

an innovative, almost sure-fire way to use this potential catastrophe to transform an angry purchaser into a committed life-long customer.

Two decades ago, one of my distributors was late in delivering 1,000 custom cabinets for one of my new products. We had already assembled our customers' systems, but now we had no cabinets in which to mount them.

I was furious because I was losing sales. I swore I would change distributors as soon as I could.

The cabinets finally arrived four weeks late, along with an invoice for $6,500, across which the distributor had scrawled, "Sorry for the delay— these first 1,000 cabinets are my treat!"

Still angry, and also in disbelief, I called the distributor and asked, "What does this mean?" He responded, "Just what it says. The cabinets are free. I failed you this time, but I still want your business!"

On hearing these words, my animosity melted. I told the distributor, "Many thanks for your gift. You have my loyalty."

And he did. Over the years, I averaged more than $20,000 in yearly orders for that same part, from that same distributor, and I stuck with him through thick and thin. He gave up a portion of his first year's profit, but he assured himself of a substantial future annuity from my company.

I remembered this favor and here's what happened when I applied the lesson to one of *my* customers. My company was located in east-central Iowa. We manufactured and distributed agricultural monitoring systems nationwide. One day I received a call about a new customer who was dissatisfied with our product. He lived just east of Indianapolis, almost a full day's drive from my office. My dealer was unable to correct the problem, so I drove over and corrected the difficulty, or so I thought.

One week later the problem reoccurred. I drove back and replaced the system with a modified console that solved the problem.

Did I lose money on that sale? Sure, but that farmer and his wife proceeded to tell every other farmer in a four-county area how fantastic our product and our service were. As a result, I sold more units in that geographical area than I did anywhere else in the country. I had managed to turn a difficult problem into a strong advertisement for the integrity of our company.

You don't always have to give away a piece of your business in order to garner the loyalty of your customers; a discount will usually do just fine. A friend told me about special-ordering a suit and experiencing a number of delays. When it finally arrived, the clothier gave him a 50 percent discount because of the difficulties. He still shops at the same clothier today.

The simple, unexpected act of providing a free (or deeply discounted) product or service when a delay on your part has caused your customer grief will result in a tenfold return of benefits in terms of profits and customer loyalty. By being creative, you, too, can turn unfortunate but inevitable service problems into golden opportunities to strengthen your business.

A final word of caution: Every so often you may be faced with "the customer from hell," a person who has a miserable home life or hates his or her job. Such customers may try to provoke you and then feed on your reaction. If you remain composed, the customer will probably calm down eventually, but if he or she continues to be offensive or crude, politely inform the person that you can't solve the problem unless there is calm. Add that, if the abuse continues, you will hang up or walk away. Then do it, if necessary. The customer will probably call back, or come back, in a more tranquil state.

How to Compete Against Giants—and Win

Shortly after my first company launched its initial product into the agri-electronics market, a major Fortune 500 company, with far more resources, unveiled a competing system. I panicked at first. Then I began to focus our company's efforts on building a strong reputation for customer service, backed by the strongest warranty program in the industry. The result? We left our Fortune 500 competitor in the dust.

A decade later, I launched a midwestern microchip company, Electronic Technology Corporation, which immediately found itself in fierce competition with several giants from California's Silicon Valley.

The foundation of our strategy, in addition to providing a top-quality product, was to develop an impressive image as the industry's leading provider of customer service, before and after the sale. We appointed a customer service manager. We installed on all our phones an unlisted phone number, dedicated to customer service. The number was released to customers only; whenever this line rang, we knew a customer wanted help. In short, we gave our customers the feeling their satisfaction was important to us, which it was.

We went on to build a multimillion-dollar backlog during our first year of operation because, fortunately for us, our competitors didn't understand what the word "service" meant.

To win the customer service game, go the extra mile. Call your customers after the sale. Ask if they are satisfied. If there is any problem in the eyes of your customer, no matter how trivial it may seem to you, fix it fast and to your customer's satisfaction—even if you lose the profit on that sale. You don't want a one-shot buyer; you want a lifetime satisfied customer.

Develop your plan of action for effective customer service by putting yourself in your customer's shoes. What kind of service would you like to see from this company? What kind of support would keep you coming back? If you can deliver that same level of service to your customers, you are destined to win the marketing game.

EXERCISE: My Customer Service Scorecard

List the strengths and weaknesses of your present customer service effort. What actions should you be taking to provide a truly outstanding level of service to your customers? When will you implement these actions?

---

*   *   *

Now that you have addressed any remaining marketing deficiencies and have completed the advanced steps in the Macrofruition process, it's time to move on to the most often overlooked—but no less essential—part of the process: the strategic activities that will shape your company's future success and ensure that the steps you've taken thus far will translate into maximized bottom-line performance.

The first step of this process involves, not just *looking* at your competitors, but for the first time *putting yourself in their shoes*, thereby gaining valuable insights into their plans for the future.

Part III
The Strategic Steps

Step Eight

Refine Your Competitive Wisdom

As the first dedicated activity of your strategic planning process, you must gather intelligence about your competitors. Only by developing an understanding of the nature, motives, and strategies of your competitors can you hope to develop meaningful strategies to compete against them effectively.

Your Intelligence System

Gathering competitive intelligence often seems like an overwhelming or impossible task, so most companies never attempt it. Most business executives relegate the subject of competitive information to the back burner, if they think to address it at all. They don't know how to go about gathering information, or they're uneasy about openly asking outsiders to provide it, so they convince themselves it's not really necessary.

If you want to win the game of business, it *is* necessary—and surprisingly easy—to learn about your competitors. You have an awesome spectrum of resources available from which to extract specific information on individual competitors.

Competitive data gathering may be accomplished by all employees who have regular contact with the outside world. Marketing and sales personnel may start the competitive-analysis ball rolling, but all employees should take part. If a secretary discovers a news article with important information on a competitor, the article should be copied and circulated to key executives. If engineers are attending a technical trade show, their duties at the show should include gathering intelligence on the competition. It is the job of all company employees to keep their eyes and ears open for competitive information.

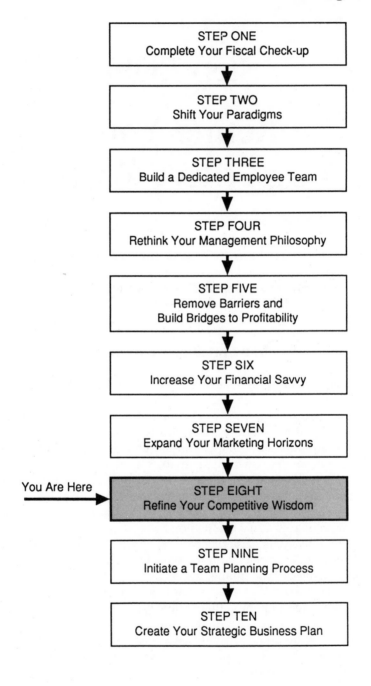

In Step Seven, you focused on the who, how, and why of your potential customers; now you must shift your in-depth focus to your competition. Initially, you'll want to determine *who* your primary competitors are; *what* they sell; *where* and *how* they sell it; *why* consumers purchase from them; and *how much* consumers purchase from them. In addition, you'll need to ascertain more about the individual companies, including the names of key executives and managers, the overall organizational structure, financial strength, special capabilities, size and location of the various facilities, sales organizations, new or anticipated products, and unique and/or proprietary designs.

With your competitors' names in hand, you can begin the intelligence-gathering process using the following tactics.

Send for competitors' product literature. Visit your library to scan trade or popular publications for articles and news releases on the companies (and ask your employees to forward to the marketing department any articles on competitive companies they may have seen). If a competitive company is publicly traded, contact a stockbroker to obtain copies of the last few annual reports (to spot trends in these companies).

Attend trade shows and visit competitors' exhibits openly (if they conceal specific products or literature when you walk in, you know what they don't want you to learn about, so find out about it later). Ask to see their products, take their literature, and invite them to your booth (and when they walk into your booth, show them what you've got and discuss features covered in your literature, but don't reveal anything you wouldn't want them to know).

Visit with distributors, dealers, sales reps, and end users about your competitors. You want to find out what they offer customers, why distributors buy from them, and how much their products sell for (wholesale and retail). If representatives from their companies are delivering formal papers, attend their presentations and ask questions from the audience.

When you meet an executive from competitive Company A, be sure to ask him or her about information on competitive companies B, C, and D. And always try to find the most senior executives from competitive companies. The more senior they are (CEOs are the best), the more freely they will expound upon their wealth of knowledge (and usually reveal far more than they should).

If you are fortunate enough to run into former employees of a competitive company, talk with them as well. Consultants are another interesting source of information. They may try to impress you with their knowledge, hoping you will hire them. (However, if they easily reveal other companies' secrets to you, don't ever consider hiring them, or you may find your own sensitive information being broadcast in a similar manner.)

In addition, contact trade and industry associations, state and local government associations (such as chambers of commerce), and—if you are computer-literate and modem-equipped—tap into the industrial databases available. However, the available database information is so vast that you will have to be selective lest you find yourself buried in reams of printed data.[1]

Make it a habit to write down key information as soon as you learn it, because you may not have a chance to visit with your source a second time.

In summary, here are some of the primary sources you can utilize as part of a legitimate intelligence-gathering system:

- Company and product literature
- Sales reps, distributors, and dealers
- End users of competitors' products
- Trade shows
- Media releases and articles (including promotions, new products, and new contracts)
- Papers and presentations by senior executives
- Annual and quarterly reports
- Stockbrokers
- Databases
- Senior company executives
- Other competitors
- Former employees of competitors
- State and local governments
- Trade and industry associations
- Trade and popular publications
- Consultants

---

1. When conducting an electronic data search, define specific key words to limit the search—words including the company name, specific divisions and products, and specific dates of interest. For example, if a company has existed for the past fifty years, you probably aren't interested in data farther back than five years. If a company is diversified (e.g., you have an electronics company, while a competitor has divisions in electronics, steel fabrication, and restaurants), use key words in your search to ensure data from irrelevant divisions of the company are not included.

EXERCISE: Who's in *Your* Competitive Closet?

Start a new page in your notebook with the heading "Competitors." List your primary competitors as you currently perceive them. Include all the relevant information you have for each competitor, such as address, location, products, and key personnel.

Next, try to list one or two other pieces of information you either suspect or recently learned about each organization. Finally, list specific sources of information you could utilize to learn more about these competitors.

Analyzing the Data

The sifting of the newly gathered data to yield an effective and timely competitive analysis is primarily a job for your marketing staff. Individual marketing staff members should be assigned individual competitors. As part of the analysis, the marketing staff should assess the companies' strengths and weaknesses; market niches; and apparent market strategies (staff should begin thinking about potential counterstrategies to use effectively against them).[2]

If analysts find holes in the data (a new mystery product or a secret process), the gaps must be filled in with reasonable assumptions, identified as such. It is surprising how the better you begin to know a competitor over time, the more accurate these educated guesses become.

Finally, each staff member should roll all of his or her data into a written report of several pages. This report should be updated every six months, with an extensive revision annually.

If possible, keep the same marketer working on the same competitor for a period of years. This allows the responsible marketer to get under the skin of the company management and to understand where it is headed.

In Appendix B, I have included an example of an actual competitive analysis, with the company identity and names changed to preserve confidentiality. Visualize this competitor (the Acme Corporation) as a primary rival of yours. Once you review this document, you will realize

---

2. An effective way to develop counterstrategies is to ask yourself how you could woo current customers away from Competitor X. To spot your own vulnerabilities, assume you are Competitor X, and develop strategies to win business away from your own company.

Figure 8-1. Example of individual company rating analysis.

Company: _____	Possible Rating Range	Rating
PERFORMANCE		
Annual sales	<$1M=1, $1M to <$10M=2, $10M to <$50M=3, $50M to <$100M=4, >$100M=5	2
Perceived strength	Poor=1, Fair=2, Average=3, Very Good=4, Excellent=5	3
Net profit	<1% Sales=0, 1 to 3% Sales=1,3 to 5%=2, 5 to 7%=3, 7% to 10%=4, >10%=5	3
Cash position	0 to 5 depending on availability of capital	2
Category average		2.5
PRODUCTS		
Product/market diversity	0 to 5 depending on diversity of products/markets	4
Product features	1 to 5 depending on richness of features	3
Product attractiveness	1 (low) to 5 (high)	3
Product ability to meet customers' needs	Poor=1, Fair=2, Average=3, Very Good=4, Excellent=5	3
Product reliability record	Poor=1, Fair=2, Average=3, Very Good=4, Excellent=5	3
Category average		3.2
AGGRESSIVENESS		
Advertising visibility	0 (no visibility) to 5 (high visibility)	4
Marketing activities	0 (no marketing) to 5 (intensive marketing)	4
Product promotions	0 (no promotions) to 5 (many promotions)	2
Product pricing	1 (priced at high end) to 5 (priced at low end)	3
Willingness to invest	1 (slight willingness) to 5 (high willingness)	2
Category average		3.0
CUSTOMER VIEWPOINT		2
Customer perception of company	Poor=1, Fair=2, Average=3, Very Good=4, Excellent=5	3
Company perception of design	Poor=1, Fair=2, Average=3, Very Good=4, Excellent=5	2
Customer perception of quality	Poor=1, Fair=2, Average=3, Very Good=4, Excellent=5	3
Strength of customer service committment	Poor=1, Fair=2, Average=3, Very Good=4, Excellent=5	2
Category average		2.5
OTHER KEY FACTORS		
Breakthrough technology	0 to 5 depending on significant breakthroughs	2
Company PR visibility in media	Poor=1, Fair=2, Average=3, Very Good=4, Excellent=5	2
Category average		2.0
COMPANY AVERAGE:	(Norm = 3.0)	2.64

that, not only do you know much more about this rival than you did before, but, more important, you can develop much more effective competitive strategies against this opponent.

Distilling the Reports

After all the individual competitive reports are completed, the marketing team needs to create a *Reader's Digest* condensation by extracting key information from each report and presenting it in comparative format in five or six key charts for strategic planning purposes. An example of the charts utilized for this competitive overview presentation is included in Appendix C. Note how information presented in this manner allows a group of senior executives to grasp the overall competitive environment very quickly.

The last chart in this briefing should be an overall ranking of your company and its primary competitors. Resist the temptation to skew the data so that your own company is always on top; you are seeking an honest assessment here. In Figure 8-1, I've included an example of a rating system I have used for this process. The ratings assume equal weighting for all categories. If you consider a particular category to be more important, multiply that category's results by a weighting factor (such as 1.5 or 2.0).

The Next Step

After all the competitive data have been gathered, condensed, and distilled, you should have a much clearer picture of your competitors' products, strategies, and capabilities. At this point, your marketing staff should review the marketing plan created in Step Seven to ascertain if any modifications need to be made in light of your additional knowledge base.

Are your marketing strategies still appropriate? Are you confident they will allow you to carve inroads into the market shares held by your rivals? Have you focused on the target niches with the most potential? (Since no company has the resources to sell to the entire world, as I stated in Step Six, it's better to tackle a few markets with excellence than to blanket the world with mediocrity.)

* * *

Armed with a revised marketing plan and a strong competitive analysis and summary, you are ready for the next step in your company's strategic planning process: the creation of your Executive Planning Team and the development of a Preliminary Operating Plan.

Step Nine

Initiate a Team Planning Process

As you begin the ninth step of the Macrofruition process, it's time to start assembling the various bricks of wisdom you have accumulated thus far into a strong foundation for your business, continuing the process of strategic planning begun in Step Eight.

Note that I said "foundation." Your intent at this stage should be to create, not a full-blown Strategic Business Plan (we'll do that in Step Ten), but rather a Preliminary Operating Plan (or POP). In this intermediate step you will develop a team comprised of your key executives to initiate the planning process; challenge them to evolve a plan of action to move the company forward; and, finally, convene an intensive two-day executive planning session at an off-site location, so that your executive team begins to think and strategize as a unified body, creating a written POP and laying the groundwork for the Strategic Business Plan to be developed later.

This strategic plan will become an operating manual for your business. The word "strategic" emphasizes the fact that this plan is absolutely critical to the success of your business. In this operating manual, you will set forth your company's objectives; describe your distinctive competence (why you will succeed); analyze your market and your competition; examine your strengths and weaknesses; and develop written strategies for achieving success. You will keep adding to the manual as your enterprise grows from a one-room shack to a multilevel mansion.

Most business executives shy away from written strategies, believing all they need is the plan that exists in their own gray matter. This is fortunate for you, because your written strategic plan will give your business the potential to speed by those without such strategies.

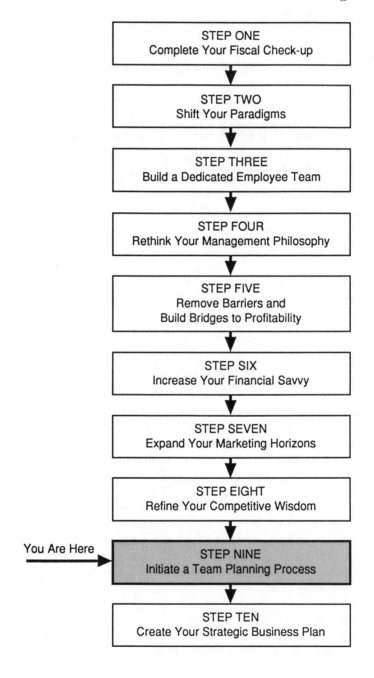

By clearly defining your strategies in writing, you lay the groundwork for all your team to follow. You will have something concrete to guide you when the going gets rough. Having a written plan also enables all team members to explain clearly your company's goals (and how they will be achieved) to potential financiers. With a strategically committed management team in place, your odds for securing financing to fuel your building efforts will be significantly enhanced.

If you use your strategic plan, you should overcome any "construction" problems you encounter. But continue hammering away without this plan, and your company will end up looking like a badly designed house that is in danger of collapse.

The Importance of Strategic Planning

You must be personally committed to the process of strategic planning before you seek the commitment of key employees. Strategic planning requires hard work, an extensive gathering of knowledge, and the application of ingenuity and imagination to interpret all the gathered data. It is not an easy process, but it is well worth the effort required. Following are some of the advantages of strategic planning:

- Strategic planning provides a clear direction for your business, helping to boost the confidence of your financiers.
- A well-defined strategic plan acts as your silent sentinel, serving as an insurance policy to guarantee the continuation of the business if you should be incapacitated; this continuity also gives confidence to your financiers.
- A strong strategic plan facilitates continued growth and effective competition through the concentration of company resources to achieve specific goals. It also helps smaller companies on limited budgets stay focused to compete against their larger competitors, many of whom lack effective strategic plans.
- The alternatives to strategic planning are far worse than the process itself. They include crisis management, knee-jerk responses to unforeseen events and pressures, and improvisational responses to problems. Although spontaneity and improvisation are important skills, especially in the short run, they are inadequate for coping with problems and potential opportunities in the long term.
- In today's rapid-paced business environment, the commercial viability of the founder's vision requires periodic review. Business

executives must guard against the complacency that sometimes follows a period of success. A periodic diagnosis of product and market trends is needed to make sound adjustments in the company's course. Think of this periodic strategic review as your company's annual "physical."

The Executive Planning Team

In many companies, strategies are developed by the chief executive and summarily announced to the rest of the staff. When a chief executive's private plan is mandated from on high, the staff may execute the plan. However, because they don't feel any ownership in its creation, they won't fervently embrace it; instead, they will work only to achieve the particular goals given to them, and nothing more.

In sharp contrast, if staff members are actively involved in the planning process and embrace a strategic plan as their own creation, they will strive to achieve all that is humanly possible, and then some.

That is why you should begin the strategic planning process by creating an Executive Planning Team (EPT). Your EPT should consist of senior executives from marketing, administration, production, and the other critical functional areas of your organization. Resist the temptation to include additional junior managers; their contribution will come later, in smaller action groups. I believe the ideal size for this team is five people, certainly no more than eight.

The EPT Kick-Off Meeting

Armed with the strategic competitive analysis completed in the previous chapter, it's time to assemble your Executive Planning Team for a meeting to kick off the planning process. During this meeting, you should:

- Explain the executive team's mission: to begin the process that will ultimately plot the strategic course of the company for the next five years.
- Explain that the executive team's job is to distill the wealth of company and competitive information into specific strategies for success and to provide the rest of the staff with the tools to implement these strategies effectively.
- Offer a list of company objectives (near-term, mid-term, and

long-term), with the clear understanding that these are tentative, for the purpose of initiating the planning process.
- Explain that the team will collectively develop specific courses of action to enable the company to achieve (and even exceed) the established objectives.
- Explain that the *two-stage mechanism* for this formative round of the strategic process will be as follows:
  1. First, you will schedule a two-day Strategic Off-Site (SOS) meeting. This will involve an intensive effort for a forty-eight-hour period, at a location remote from the office, without spouses. The result of the SOS will be a draft planning document known as the Preliminary Operating Plan, or POP (these activities will be covered in this chapter).
  2. Following the SOS, subcommittees will be formed to resolve any remaining action items; then a scheduled multimonth planning process will be instituted that will culminate in the adoption of a formal Strategic Business Plan (SBP) for the company (the SBP is covered in Step Ten).

Planning the Strategic Off-Site Meeting

After the EPT kick-off meeting, you should begin planning the Strategic Off-Site (SOS) meeting. Keep the details closely held (ideally between you and your executive assistant), releasing only small pieces of information at a time. In this manner, you will keep your executives focused on the results, not on the process.

Your SOS should be productive and exciting, but it can also be very stressful, as different well-intentioned ideologies clash in an intense environment. Because of this stress, I recommend that some enjoyable activities (and even some amusing surprises) be scheduled to provide a safety valve. I'll discuss these further when I outline the specifics of the SOS.

Start by selecting two tentative meeting dates, both four to six weeks in the future. A Thursday-to-Friday combination (which involves arriving Wednesday evening) is ideal, because your EPT members will have the weekend to consider follow-up actions from the SOS.

Contact several hotels and resorts at least one hour's drive from your facility. Reserve a room for each member of the team, as well as a meeting room for the entire period. Make sure there are informal activities available after hours: swimming, volleyball, exercising.

Tentatively block both sets of dates with the facility. Then contact each member of your team, offering the choice of dates, and pick the one most team members prefer (but which all can attend). Then book the date and sign the contract with the facility.

The meeting room at the facility should be equipped with the following: blackboard, flip charts, overhead projector, a separate area for food and refreshments, and a round (or square) table that lets everyone face everyone else, with plenty of room. The room should be private, with no folding temporary walls separating it from adjacent rooms, because voices will be raised from time to time during the SOS. Also, unless all of your team members are avid smokers, I highly recommend a nonsmoking environment for the meeting room (smokers can take breaks out in the hall).

You'll also want to arrange the following with the sales department (and/or a nearby facility):

The evening before
7:00-9:00 P.M.: Open bar and snacks in a private area by the pool (or in an area pub close by).

First day in the meeting room
7:30 A.M.: Continental breakfast in the meeting room.
9:45 A.M.: Tidy up break table and refresh beverages for 10:00 A.M. break.
11:45 A.M.: Bring in lunch consisting of deli sandwiches, etc.
2:00 P.M.: Bring in soft drinks and snacks.

First day—evening
Poolside pizza party, if you can have relative privacy (or pizza party at nearby establishment, if it has a semiprivate area), to release tensions of the day.

Second day in the meeting room
Same as first day, except different lunch.

Second day—evening
Closing banquet with open bar (at resort or facility nearby).

Although it won't be on the official agenda, schedule one or more unanticipated entertaining diversions during the SOS—events that will

Figure 9-1. Timetable of handouts in advance of SOS.

When	What
Three or four weeks before SOS	Send memo to EPT members with dates for SOS.
Two weeks before SOS	Distribute assessment questionnaire to each member of EPT (see Figure 9-2).
One week before SOS	EPT members return completed assessment questionnaire to your administrative assistant.
Three days before SOS	Distribute memo to EPT members with preliminary agenda (Figure 9-3).
Upon departing for SOS	Distribute folder to each EPT member with final detailed agenda (Figure 9-4) and consolidated questionnaire results.

temporarily take participants' minds off the task at hand.[1] These might include a spontaneous visit by a singing group of actors in costume, or a short skit by a bogus visiting executive from a competitive company to discuss, tongue-in-cheek, his or her perspective on your company. The idea is to present something totally unexpected that will bring some laughs and smiles for fifteen minutes before your staff returns to the hard work of creative planning.

Handouts

When all the arrangements have been made, there are a number of handouts to provide to the team before the SOS. Figure 9-1 shows the chronological order in which you should distribute these handouts.

1. There is a sound basis for this activity. You want to maximize productivity in a short time period. Studies conducted on pilots undergoing accelerated flight training ground school during World War II show that if, at several times during the intensive training sessions, the pilots' activities were temporarily diverted to an entirely different, and enjoyable, task, their overall productivity was significantly enhanced when they returned to their training.

Three or four weeks before the SOS. At this time you should send a memo to your team members letting them know the dates selected for the SOS and reminding them that their attendance will be required from Wednesday evening through Friday evening. Don't reveal the location yet, in order to keep the anticipation building.

Two weeks before the SOS. Provide each member of the EPT with an assessment questionnaire to be completed within one week and returned to your administrative assistant (refer to the example in Figure 9-2). The candid answers of each team member will provide fodder for the discussions during the SOS.

One week before the SOS. Each team member returns his or her completed questionnaire to your administrative assistant, who compiles all questionnaire responses into a composite (without identifying respondents) to be used as a handout.

EXERCISE: Your Assessment of Your Company

Review the Assessment Questionnaire (Figure 9-2). Start a new page in your notebook, and write short concise answers to each of the assessment questions as they apply to your vision of your business.

Three days before the SOS. Distribute a memo to team members containing a preliminary agenda. This memo identifies the meeting location and informs team members that the dress is casual. See Figure 9-3 for an example of the preliminary SOS agenda. The ideal way to arrange transportation is to rent a minivan so that the team can travel together; this keeps the creative juices flowing (before and after).

Inform the team member from the marketing department that he or she will be required to present the competitive assessment mid-morning on the first day, lead a subsequent discussion on the implications of the competition for your company, and discuss several options and alternatives. The time allotted for this portion of the SOS will be slightly less than two hours.

Determine the most appropriate team member to act as scribe for the meeting. Ensure that the chosen scribe brings along a laptop computer or other materials to record the relevant details of each session.

Upon departing for the SOS. Your executive assistant will have prepared a folder for each team member, with the attendee's name on the

Figure 9-2. Assessment questionnaire.

Team Member: _____
                        (name)

(Use additional sheets for your answers, but provide no more than
two or three sentences to answer each question.)

1. What is your perception of where we are now
   A. With the planned growth of our company?
   B. With our understanding of the business we're in and the market we serve?
   C. With our business capabilities and the ability to seize new opportunities?

2. What is your perception of where our competitors are
   A. With respect to their present product lines?
   B. With respect to anticipated new developments and products?
   C. With respect to their probable business strategies?

3. Do you believe we should
   A. Expand existing markets, pursue new ones, or both? Why?
   B. Become more aggressive or more conservative with our sales projections
      and market assumptions? Why?
   C. Expand or modify our company goals? Why?

4. Given your vision of what our company could be, what should we do to get there
   A. In terms of new, modified, and/or retained strategies?
   B. In terms of new, modified, and/or retained resources?

5. How can we make it happen
   A. In terms of organizational structure changes or additions?
   B. In terms of staffing changes or additions?

6. How can we effectively monitor results
   A. By tracking existing company schedules and priorities?
   B. By establishing new schedules, priorities, or committees?
   C. Through existing company budgets and controls?
   D. By establishing new budgets and control systems?

front. These folders are given to team members as they depart for the
SOS. In this folder, include a final, detailed agenda (see Figure 9-4),
copies of the team member's completed questionnaire, and a copy of the
consolidated questionnaire results. Also include a writing pad and any
other material you deem pertinent (for example, copies of prior business

Figure 9-3. Example of preliminary SOS agenda handout sheet.

Our Strategic Off-Site (SOS) meeting will be held Thursday and Friday, May 10-11, at the Pines Resort in Center City. All meetings will take place in a designated conference room that will be indicated in the handout material you will receive Wednesday afternoon. Dress will be casual (bring swimming gear), and all meals will be provided.

Working materials will be provided, so you need bring only resource material that may be of help. A copy of your original assessment questionnaire response and a composite of all responses will be in the folder you will receive at the start of the conference.

The mission of our SOS is to develop the foundation for a strong strategic plan for our company, so we want no outside interruptions. For this reason, spouses will not be accompanying the team. Also, because of the importance of this off-site meeting, we urge you to limit phone calls back to the office to dire emergencies only. Please coordinate these through my executive assistant. Inform your spouse (not coworkers) that the facility phone number is 123-4567.

Our van will depart from the office promptly at 5:00 P.M. Wednesday and will arrive back at the office by 10:00 P.M. Friday. (Alternate: Please plan to arrive and be checked in by no later than 7:00 P.M. Wednesday. We will arrive home late Friday evening.)

SOS Agenda

WEDNESDAY, May 9

(Complete check-in prior to 7:00 P.M.)
7:00 P.M. - 9:00 P.M.: Open bar and hors d'oeuvres (location: poolside)

THURSDAY, May 10

7:30 A.M.: Continental breakfast in meeting room
8:00 A.M.: SOS convenes
Noon-12:30 P.M.: Lunch in meeting room
7:00 P.M.: Adjourn meeting
7:00 P.M. - ?: Pizza dinner and review (location: poolside)

FRIDAY, May 11

7:30 A.M.: Continental breakfast in meeting room
8:00 A.M.: SOS reconvenes
Noon-12:30 P.M.: Lunch in meeting room
4:45 P.M.: Adjourn meeting
5:00 P.M.: Closing banquet
9:00 P.M.: Van departs for office

plans, financial statements, pro formas, product descriptions, and past vision statements and objectives).

The detailed agenda contains more specific information than the preliminary handout. It is set up in the same format as the assessment questionnaire because the purpose of the questionnaire was to pose strategic questions and the purpose of the SOS is to answer those questions as a group.

Figure 9-4. Example of formal detailed SOS agenda.

SOS Agenda

WEDNESDAY, May 9
7:00 P.M. - 9:00 P.M.: Poolside kickoff meeting (leave folders in room)

THURSDAY, May 10
7:30 A.M.: Continental breakfast in meeting room (bring folders)
8:00 A.M.: SESSION I—WHERE ARE WE NOW? (Leader: President)
10:00 A.M.: SESSION II—WHERE IS OUR COMPETITION? (Leader: Marketing)
Noon: Lunch in meeting room
12:30 P.M.: SESSION III—WHERE DO WE WANT TO GO? (Facilitator: President)
7:00 P.M.: Evening meeting review and pizza dinner (location: poolside or ?)

FRIDAY, May 11
7:30 A.M.: Continental breakfast in meeting room (bring folders)
8:00 A.M.: Sessions begin
SESSION IV—HOW DO WE GET THERE? (Facilitator: President)
SESSION V—WHO IS RESPONSIBLE? (Facilitator: President)
SESSION VI—HOW DO WE MONITOR RESULTS? (Facilitator: President)
4:45 P.M.: Adjourn meeting
5:00 P.M.: Closing banquet (location: ?)
9:00 P.M.: Van departs for office

All material for this meeting (handouts, charts, personal notes, etc.) should be considered to be COMPANY CONFIDENTIAL material and treated as such.

Making the SOS Work

As the chief executive, you must ensure that the planning team works and plays together, building a consensus instead of breaking into small cliques. During all of the forthcoming meetings (not including the evening get-togethers), you should act as facilitator to keep the discussion centered on the topic at hand, not allowing digressions into side issues. When side issues arise, suggest that they be either tabled for one of the other sessions or assigned for a subcommittee during Session IV. Keep your team focused on the task that lies before it (with the exception of the previously discussed short "fun" diversions) so that you can achieve meaningful results in two days.

The Evening Before

The first evening's get-together should start with an overview of the ground rules:

- Everyone should be at all sessions on time.
- There is to be no smoking in the meeting room (inform smokers of smoking area).
- Participants should expect hard work, because they will be building the foundation for the company's future.
- Everyone should get a good night's rest and be ready to go early; all team members should be at the conference room for breakfast by 7:30 the next morning.

The rest of the evening is formal, except that you might want to bring up several topics of interest for discussion, based on the results of the questionnaires completed by team members.

The First Day

Session I—Where Are We Now? This session is two hours in duration including a short break.

President's opening remarks. This is your senior executive pep talk. Discuss the exciting threshold that lies before the team. Note that this meeting begins a rebirth for the company through the achievement of a unity of purpose and plan, with everyone willing to provide both give and take in order to evolve success strategies all team members can embrace.

Explain to the team members that hard work lies ahead and that the future success of the company is in their hands. Reiterate that this off-site meeting will build a strong foundation for the eventual execution of a strategic business plan that will guide the company's future growth.

Explain that you will be standing in front of the team only for the first session. From that point on, your role will be that of a facilitator, to help the team reach a consensus. Identify the official scribe for the SOS.

Let the team know that it will develop specific short-term and long-term strategies for the company during the course of the SOS. State that it will be the team's responsibility to implement those strategies and to ensure that company resources are effectively utilized in order to achieve key strategic objectives.

2. *Company vision statement.* The focus of an overriding company vision statement is important for the SOS team. If the company currently has a vision statement—a paragraph or so that clearly articulates the company's reason for being—it should be discussed. The team should decide whether the stated vision truly reflects the focus of the company. If not, team members should take some time now to modify it so that it more closely resembles the collective vision of team members. If a vision statement does not exist, the team should draft a statement to serve as a focal point for the SOS.[2]

The vision statement may undergo significant changes as a result of the discussions that will take place at the SOS. The idea is, not to produce the final version of the vision statement right now, but to provide the team with a starting point for the discussions that will follow over the next two days.[3]

Write the agreed-upon SOS vision statement on flip-chart paper, and tape it to the wall for all to see during next two days.

Here is an example of a manufacturing company's SOS vision statement:

> Acme Technology Corporation is dedicated to supplying the highest quality monitoring systems to its customers, with a firm commitment to reliability, customer service, and profitability.

3. *Summary of the past, present, and future.* If you have a prior written plan or list of strategic objectives, hand out copies and discuss past objectives, successes, and failures. Review the nature of your business, not just from the perspective of building widgets, but also from the perspective of satisfying a consumer need and improving the quality of life.

Discuss the present and anticipated business environment, your current capabilities, and potential opportunities.

---

2. An excellent source for the preparation of a vision statement is the *Vision Statement Guide* available from Jan Cook Reicher Associates, 313 First Street, Hoboken, N.J. 07030. (Send a check for $4.00 and a self-addressed envelope pre-stamped for two ounces.)
3. Effective company vision statements can take months to create. If a draft vision statement must be created for the SOS, a committee should be formed after the SOS to complete the evolution of the draft into a final vision statement.

Session II—Where Is Our Competition? This session is two hours in length, including a short break at the end. It begins with an overview of the strategic competitive analysis that the marketing department prepared earlier (see Appendix C). It evolves into a discussion of the top three or four competitors and where the team expects them to go, as well as what new products the EPT expects them to offer. In this forum, challenges may be issued to the marketing department's assessments, based on additional perspectives from the other team members.

Next, the team should utilize the flip chart or the overhead projector to complete the Competitive Posture chart shown in Figure 9-5.

Names of individual competitors (or in some cases individual competitors' product names) are inserted onto the chart as rectangles, on the basis of current state of maturity and perceived competitive position. Your company's products are inserted as circles on the chart (you may choose to use different colors or different shapes for each competitor). In addition, add trend arrows showing the general direction in which you believe a particular product or competitor is heading. (Your chart may have more objects than are shown in this figure.)

Following are examples of the status of selected products and competitors in Figure 9-5:

- Our Product A is emerging from an embryonic state with a strong growth projection and is already viewed favorably relative to the competition.

- Conversely, our Product C is a mature product with a current strong competitive position; however, its popularity has peaked, and it is predicted to undergo a competitive slide.

- Competitor D's product line is just emerging from an embryonic state but is already enjoying a strong competitive position. Although its popularity appears to have peaked, sales are predicted to remain competitively flat for the future.

Post this chart on the wall of the meeting room, where it can be utilized for future session discussions. The completed chart gives you a picture of where your products are relative to those of the competition.

This session should conclude with a review of recommended marketing strategies and the possible development of additional strategies, covering the areas of advertising, promotions, products, pricing, and service that will have the most significant impact on the competition.

Figure 9-5. Competitive posture: us vs. them.

Competitive Position →	State of Maturity →			
	Embryonic	Growth	Mature	Aging
Leading		Competitor A		
Strong	Competitor D →	Our Product C		
Favorable	Our Product A	Our Product B	Competitor C →	
Tenable				
Weak	Competitor B			

Source: Adapted from a concept called The 3M Planning System. See M. Tita and R. Allio. "3M's Strategy System—Planning an Innovative Organization," *Planning Review XII* (1984), pp. 10–15.

Session III—Where Do We Want to Go? This session occupies all afternoon, from four to six hours with a mid-afternoon break, until a natural completion point is reached. Begin with a recap of your business and market environments. Expand this into a discussion of the company's strengths and weaknesses.

After some initial discussion, develop a blackboard chart (see Figure 9-6) that relates your company strengths and weaknesses to business or market threats and opportunities.

Individual entries tie a particular strength or weakness to a threat or opportunity. Note that your chart will have far more individual entries than this example. When this chart is complete, it should be posted on the wall of the meeting room as a reference.

Next, assess your individual product lines as they contribute to your business strengths. Factors that influence this assessment include your technical and/or manufacturing advantages, price competitiveness, your relative market share, and the level of customer acceptance of the product.

Figure 9-6. Company vs. business environment matrix.

	◄——————— Business Environment ———————►	
	Threats	Opportunities
Company Strengths	Although we are the leader in agricultural monitoring systems, we do not have development budget of some newer competitors. + (others)	Our Product A could be expanded into a new niche: the home security market. + (others)
Company Weaknesses	Our field sales force does not have effective promotional material to keep up with competition. + (others)	Our Product B is too expensive; we should position as a top quality unit with stronger warranty. + (others)

Next, looking at these same product lines, assess the attractiveness of the markets your are targeting. Factors to consider in this assessment include overall market size, growth rate of the market, profit margins that can be realized if you sell your product in this market at a competitive price, barriers to entry in the market, and level of competition.

Armed with these data, you should create a final matrix chart that displays your business strengths in terms of your individual product families. (A sample chart is shown in Figure 9-7.)

Figure 9-7. Our product family strength vs. industry attractiveness.

Industry Attractiveness ▼	◄——————— Our Business Strength ———————►		
	Strong	Average	Weak
High		Our Product A	
Medium		Our Product B	
Low			Our Product C

Each of your product lines should be inserted into the chart as a circle, positioned according to your assessment of its business strength and industry attractiveness. Here, too, add a trend arrow showing what you believe to be the general direction in which a particular product is heading. Your chart should have more objects than shown in this example, but not as many as your competitive analysis chart.

Here is an explanation of Our Product A in Figure 9-7: Product A enjoys high industry attractiveness (on the basis of an overview of market size, growth rate, and profit margin categories) and average business strength (on the basis of an overall average of its technical/manufacturing advantages, competitive pricing, market share, and customer acceptance). It continues to trend toward even greater business strength.

The completed chart gives you a clear picture of your product line strengths relative to the marketplace. Post this chart on the wall of the meeting room with the others.

In the future, you will be preparing updated versions of these trend charts (Figures 9-5 and 9-7) on an annual basis. Comparisons to previous charts will help you to see long-term trends.

Use the completed data and the discussion thus far to develop a list of key success factors (both short-term and long-term). Write these on a flip-chart sheet, and post them on the wall.

Develop a list of the assumptions utilized in developing the sales forecasts. List and categorize additional opportunities (areas where you might exceed forecast) as well as risks (areas where you might fall short of forecast). Transfer these data to the flip-chart sheets, and add the sheets to the family of accumulating wall charts.

Discuss additional product possibilities, and agree on the overall product emphasis (both near-term and long-term).

If you have time, start to develop a chart defining specific company objectives as the team now sees them. Keep this chart on the flip-chart stand.

For security reasons, it is important that, at the conclusion of the meeting, all charts be covered for the night. Either take them down, or tape blank sheets over them until the following morning. And reiterate that, because all notes are considered company confidential, no written material should be thrown into the wastebasket. Any material to be discarded should be taken back to the office, where it can be shredded or burned.

The Evening Review. After a break of no more than an hour, the team should reconvene for an evening consisting of an informal bull session and a casual dinner. You want a semiprivate area so that informal but confidential discussions may continue and additional creative ideas can surface. Try to wrap up by 10:00 P.M. so that everyone will be fresh in the morning.

The Second Day

Be sure all charts are again posted and visible. This day consists of three sessions. You should schedule these at your own pace, with the first session being the lengthiest (probably four to five hours).

Session IV—How Do We Get There? The structure for this session is determined by the previous day's events and by the momentum at the conclusion of the previous session. If the development of the company objectives was not completed, this effort should be continued until the team is satisfied. Then this chart should be posted on the wall.

Next, the team should review the vision statement posted the previous morning. Does the statement still reflect the correct focus? If not, now is the time to change it.

Next, marketing staff members should lead a discussion of sales projections for the next five years. The team should be satisfied that these projections are still valid in light of the team's agreed-upon product emphasis and company direction.

The remainder of this session should be spent discussing strategy formulation and the resources (in terms of dollars and people) needed to ensure success. The strategies discussed may include pricing, market niches, distribution, manufacturing, and administration. Nothing should be considered sacred. The discussion may lead to resource reallocation (or additions) in terms of people, capital, and space. You must have in hand a set of definitive strategies for success at the conclusion of this session.

There will be a number of issues yet to be resolved at the conclusion of this session, and subcommittees will need to be formed at the company (utilizing additional staff members) to resolve these issues. Some time should be spent discussing the membership and leadership of these committees, the finalizing of which will take place in the next session.

Session V—Who Is to Be Responsible? Even the most exciting program won't happen by itself; people make things happen. In this session, the team will determine who will be responsible for allocating resources and implementing each of the strategies and for setting implementation timelines. The team will make a final determination as to the responsibilities and makeup of the committees, develop written statements of their individual charters, and determine the time frames for carrying out their charters. Finally, the team will decide which EPT members will be responsible for overseeing the committees.

The committees can then be officially created by executive memorandum on the next working day (Monday), so the committees can hit the ground running that week and report back to their designated EPT members in a timely manner.

Session VI—How Do We Monitor Results? In this wrap-up session, the team needs to establish a firm overall implementation schedule for each of the monitored activities. If resources are tight, priorities must be established. Initial budgets for implementation, subject to assessment by the board of directors, need to be proposed.

A set of control systems needs to be established to ensure that newly proposed strategic activities will work smoothly within the company and to ensure that all employees will work to achieve new objectives, rather than trying to sabotage them.

Closing Banquet. The team has earned this one, so let your hair down and have fun for a few hours before returning to your families.

Keeping the Ball Rolling

When you return to the office, ensure that the action committees are formed and that they begin meetings quickly. Be sure to continue discussions on open SOS items at executive staff meetings.

As soon as possible, have the results of the SOS meeting (as recorded by your designated scribe) transcribed into an official Preliminary Operating Plan (with an appropriate Company Confidential cover sheet). Distribute copies to team members for reference. Include a cover letter reiterating that this is the first stage of your strategic planning process, with the second stage to follow soon (see Step Ten). Then track the results of the committees to a successful conclusion, and follow through to ensure implementation of the agreed-upon strategies from the SOS.

EXERCISE: Timetable for *Your* SOS

Write down options in your notebook for your Company's first SOS.

1. Make a list of adequate facilities that are at least one hour from your office.
2. Given the scheduling proposed in this chapter, when would be a good time to hold your SOS?
3. In what ways would you modify the SOS agenda proposed in this chapter?
4. Are there any other issues specific to your business that you would like to have addressed at your SOS?

---

*   *   *

This step involved the formation of an Executive Planning Team, which developed a concise written Preliminary Operating Plan for your company. What awaits is the final step—factoring in specific sales, risks, and road maps and condensing the result into a handful of charts known as the Strategic Business Plan, which is critical if you are to maximize the long-term profit success of your company.

Step Ten

Create Your Strategic Business Plan

Throughout the course of previous chapters, you have gathered most of the pieces needed to develop your strategic business plan. All that remains is to assemble the pieces into a coherent strategy—the focus of Step Ten.

The Strategic Business Plan

The classic business plan contains information about the company, its management team, its product(s), and its marketing and financial strategies. It is usually created as a tool to raise capital.

The Strategic Business Plan (or SBP) is different. It focuses on those actions necessary to achieve continued success and plots the company's course for the future, usually the next five years.

Compare a chief executive operating without a strategic business plan to a person driving a car at night in a thick fog. The only vision the driver has is the small portion of road illuminated by the car's headlights. The purpose of a strategic business plan is to clear away the fog so the pathway to success can be seen.

The Strategic Off-Site session you conducted with your key executives (Step Nine) yielded a written Preliminary Operating Plan that serves as the launching pad from which to create your SBP. If you are the CEO of a very small company, the SBP may be created by the same executives who were part of the Executive Planning Team. However, if your company has additional functional managers and key personnel, these employees should be integrated into the SBP planning team process.

171

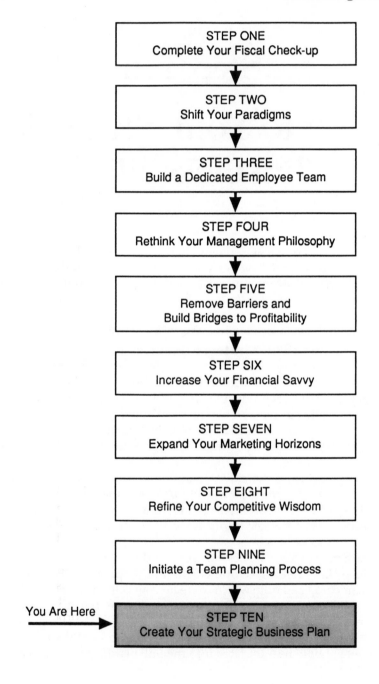

So that you understand just how an SBP differs from the POP you created in Step Nine, the next section presents a typical completed SBP. The rest of the chapter describes the process you should utilize within your company to create your own SBP charts and the preferred way to develop your SBP.

A Typical SBP

The content of each company's SBP is unique, taking into account many industry-specific, market-specific, and company-specific factors. Whatever the content, I suggest you develop your SBP in the form of a series of charts, rather than as formal written text. By doing so, you create a document that can be reviewed quickly, both now and in the future. A plan developed in this manner is easier to comprehend and more likely to be implemented than a written plan that is two inches thick.

A typical SBP might include a dozen charts similar to those described on the following pages. The example is for a fictitious company, Apex Corporation, that manufactures monitoring systems and security systems. The concepts can be readily adapted to your company, regardless of business type. It is my intent, not to present a strict, inflexible format, but rather to familiarize you with the process and the assumptions underlying the SBP so that you can develop your own unique set of charts.

Assembly of the SBP begins at the lowest level of profit center in the company—the business segment. Different companies define their business segments differently. For example, a company with multiple product lines (e.g., products for home use and products for automotive use) will probably define each line as a business segment. If there is just one product line but several different markets (e.g., wholesale, retail, and direct mail), each of the markets may represent a business segment. If there are multiple product lines and several distinct markets with different marketing or other requirements, each product-market combination may represent a business segment.

First, a set of SBP charts is prepared for each business segment. Then, the information in the individual business segment charts is consolidated into a companywide SBP (if the company is fairly small, with just a single business segment, this step is not required). The Apex Corporation charts on the following pages represent a companywide, consolidated SBP. (Note that in the Strategic Road Map—Chart 9—Apex has seven distinct business segments.)

Chart 1: Agenda. This chart contains the primary SBP presentation headings. Each heading represents a separate chart.

Apex SBP Agenda
- Objectives
- Markets
- Global Considerations
- Market Opportunities
- Competitive Analysis
- Business Base/Focus
- Key Issues
- Strategic Road Map
- Factored Sales
- Risks and Opportunities
- Summary

Chart 2: Objectives.[1] This chart presents a list of your business objectives, which may also include your vision statement.

Apex Objectives
- Broaden our existing monitoring system product base through selective market penetration in new growth areas.
- Utilize our technology to develop a new line of monitoring systems for the medical industry.
- Develop a strategic alliance with an international marketing partner to expand our markets in Europe and the Pacific Rim.
- Expand our sales by at least 40 percent during the five-year period.

Apex Vision Statement
We are dedicated to supplying the highest quality monitoring systems to our customers, with a firm commitment to reliability, customer service, and profitability.

---

1. These objectives, strategies, and tactics portions are very similar to their counterparts in the marketing plan discussed in Step Seven, except that we are no longer looking at only a marketing perspective, but rather an overall company plan of action. Therefore these objectives include marketing, manufacturing, financial, and administrative goals.

Chart 3: Markets. In this chart, list your company's markets in a variety of ways: traditional markets and growth markets, as well as customers (present and future) by name, type, or territory.

Apex Markets	
Traditional	*Growth*
• Industrial Monitoring	• Hospital and Clinic Monitoring
• Traffic Monitoring	• Industrial Security
• Residential Security	• Military Security
Present Major Customers	*Future Customer Targets*
• John Deere	• Medical Electronics Supply Centers
• McDonnell Douglas	• Major Business Security Dealers
• Trailmobile	• Department of Defense
• NASA	
• Municipal Governments	
• Home Security Distributors	

Chart 4: Global Considerations. This chart contains major factors that will influence the growth of your sales, such as the environment, trends in the marketplace, technology drivers,[2] and the competitive climate.

Apex Global Considerations	
Business Environment	*Market Trends*
• Recessionary economy and budget cutbacks	• Strong user desire for equipment to lower operating costs
• Industrial users striving to increase production capacity without additional expense	• End users moving from corporate to divisional decisions
• Fuel cost increases mandating more efficient traffic routing	• Integration of previously separate functions into single unit
• Increasing military security funds	

2. Technology drivers are new innovations in products, marketing, manufacturing, or general business operation that have the potential to affect your orders and profits on a broad scale.

• Residential crime increasing	• Modular equipment designed for easy upgrades and extended lifetimes
Technology Drivers	*Competitive Climate*
• Color flat panel displays with graphics and video	• More electronics companies expanding into monitoring
• Touch-screen operation	• Fewer/stronger competitors in medical monitoring marketplace
• User-friendly software and diagnostics	
• Optical disk memory storage	• End-users complain about slow equipment service
• Auto-calibration/rapid setup	• Competitors offering discounts to close orders
	• Joint ventures more prevalent

I have shown global considerations on a single chart. However, if you have a large number of global considerations (and you should), consider a separate chart for each business segment or market (such as one chart for the global considerations associated with industrial monitoring, another chart for traffic monitoring, another for residential security, and so on).

Chart 5: Market Opportunities. This chart lists market opportunities deriving from the global considerations presented in Chart 4. For example, if you have a drought-resistant lawn turf product, a dry summer may influence sales; if you have created a bacterium that eats oil sludge, newly allocated federal funds for environmental clean-up could affect orders. List these market opportunities.

Apex Market Opportunities

• Develop modular packaging to offer several of our present individual industrial systems in a single, upgradable product.
• Accelerate new military security system to offer off-the-shelf for upcoming government security system programs.
• Offer new medical monitoring system that reduces nurse/patient ratio in intensive care.
• Create new line of residential systems with wireless transmission to central station.

Chart 6: Competitive Analysis. In this chart, update the consolidated data compiled for (and reviewed at) your Strategic Off-Site meeting and discussed in detail in Step Nine.

Apex Competitive Analysis[3]

- Competitor Beta is rated highest by users in customer service, and we are a strong second. Beta also has the highest average price, while we are second.
- Competitor Delta is the leader in medical monitoring, and Sigma is the leader in military monitoring.
- Alpha is the only competitor that has begun to enter overseas markets; however, it is rumored that Beta and Delta are looking for international teaming partners.
- None of our competitors offers a wireless transmission to central station capability similar to the one we have developed.
- Delta is the only competitor offering a modular packaging concept.
- The least competitive markets are hospitals, military security, and international industrial monitoring.
- The most competitive markets are U.S. residential monitoring and industrial monitoring.

Chart 7: Business Base/Focus. This chart contains a description of your product focus (segmented by product type and/or customer need).

Apex Business Base/Focus

- The "Sentry" Series 1000 Industrial Monitoring System Line
- The "Sentinel" Series 2000 Traffic Monitoring System Line
- The "Home Guard" Series 3000 Residential Security System Line
- The New "Guardian" Series 6000 Medical Monitoring System Line
- The Proposed "Silent Sentry" Series 8000 Industrial Security System Line
- The Proposed "Silent Watch" Series 9000 Military Security System Line

---

3. Some companies utilize code names for their key competitors (Alpha, Beta, Delta,and Sigma in this chart) to protect this sensitive information from prying eyes.

Chart 8: Key Issues. This chart delineates by product or business segment those key issues that could have an impact on the successful achievement of sales (e.g., a competitor's introduction of a lower-cost product or the impending scarcity of a particular raw material you utilize).

Apex Key Issues

Industrial Monitoring/Security

- Must reduce costs to compete with new competition.
- Must convince users the new modular concept will save money.
- Solve problem of touch screen in dirty environment.

Residential Security

- Achieve lower cost for higher market share.
- Develop more effective retail product distribution and service.
- Current wireless technology approaching saturation.

Traffic Monitoring

- Lower-cost rugged sensor needed for traffic detection.
- Educate user on advantages of lower life-cycle cost systems.
- Develop effective new-technology demonstrator.

Medical Monitoring

- New product unproven.
- No medical marketing presence.
- End users loyal to present brands.

Military Security

- Lack production hardware.
- Lack key customers contacts.
- Develop understanding of military proposal process and strategies.

Chart 9: Strategic Road Map. This chart is a graphic representation of how your different products will evolve and interact (by providing an expanding knowledge base, design insights/improvements, or marketing input for other products) during the next five-year period.

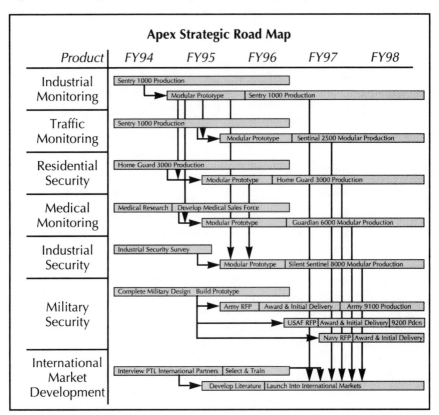

Chart 10: Factored Sales. This sales chart includes probability factors for each projected sale and may include an additional task or discount for the first year's total sales (these elements will be explained in detail in the section "Development of Five-Year Sales Projections").

	Factor (%)	FY94	FY95	FY96	FY97	FY98
Product Line #1						
Customer A Sales	80	$224,000	$ 248,000	$ 264,000	$ 272,000	$ 280,000
Customer B Sales	60	96,000	114,000	132,000	150,000	168,000
Customer C Sales	50	45,000	55,000	65,000	75,000	85,000
Customer D Sales	70	0	56,000	112,000	168,000	224,000
Product Line #2						
Customer A Sales	50	$ 0	$ 90,000	$ 90,000	$ 0	$ 0
Customer D Sales	80	136,000	184,000	200,000	216,000	232,000
Customer E Sales	60	0	90,000	108,000	126,000	144,000
Product Line #3						
Customer B Sales	70	$ 35,000	$ 70,000	$ 112,000	$ 154,000	$ 196,000
Customer F Sales	80	32,000	64,000	96,000	128,000	168,000
Customer G Sales	70	0	42,000	77,000	112,000	133,000
Totals		$568,000	$1,013,000	$1,256,000	$1,401,000	$1,630,000

Chart 11: Risks and Opportunities. There may be additional risks and opportunities (also referred to as Rs and Os) that are not reflected on your factored sales chart—for example, a company may not exercise an option you've given it to purchase a product in bulk at a discounted rate, or a large order may be terminated. You need an additional chart to reflect such potential risks, as well as potential opportunities.

To generate this supplemental chart, play a "what if" game, assuming a variety of potential scenarios that may have an additional positive effect (opportunities) or negative effect (risks) on your sales projections. This chart presents a typical representation of Rs and Os.[4]

---

4. The designators A-1, E-2, F-3, etc., refer to the *customer* (example: Customer A) and the *product line* (example: Product Line #1) from Chart 10. Individual lines specify orders, programs, or customers, depending on the nature of the risk or opportunity (e.g., "Program G-3 Terminated" refers to the termination of the program associated with Customer G and Product Line #3).

Risks and Opportunities

	FY94	FY95	FY96	FY97	FY98
Risks					
Drop Order A-1 Options	$ 0	($ 90,000)	($ 90,000)	$ 0	$ 0
Program B-1 Growth Eliminated	0	(30,000)	(60,000)	(90,000)	(120,000)
Lose Customer E-2 Downselect	0	(150,000)	(180,000)	(210,000)	(240,000)
Program G-3 Terminated	0	(60,000)	(110,000)	(160,000)	(190,000)
Order F-3 Downsized	0	(16,000)	(32,000)	(48,000)	(64,000)
Program B-3 Slips One Year	(35,000)	(35,000)	(42,000)	(42,000)	(42,000)
	($ 35,000)	($ 381,000)	($ 514,000)	($ 550,000)	($ 656,000)
Opportunities					
Customer C-1 Int'l Expansion	$ 10,000	$ 40,000	$ 50,000	$ 60,000	$ 70,000
Customer A-1 Add'l Markets	0	20,000	50,000	80,000	110,000
Program D-1 Goes Sole-Source	0	50,000	110,000	165,000	215,000
Program H (1999) Accelerates	0	0	0	120,000	230,000
Cost Breakthrough on Order B-1	32,000	38,000	44,000	50,000	56,000
New Customer J-3	0	50,000	90,000	130,000	170,000
	$ 42,000	$ 198,000	$ 344,000	$ 605,000	$ 851,000

Chart 12: Summary. This final chart consists of four to six key summation points representing the most critical elements of your SBP.

Apex Summary

- Lower-cost modular product designs are essential for continued growth and success.
- Newly developed wireless design creates additional opportunities for existing products.
- Timely completion of new military security system affords access to upcoming military RFPs and strengthens win probability.
- New medical monitoring line should have immediate market acceptance with its ability to reduce medical personnel workload significantly.
- Timely international partner selection and development, coupled with international product literature, opens lucrative new markets.
- Because customer service is critical to our success, we must improve our level of customer service to ensure we achieve the #1 position compared to our competition.

The SBP Process

Now that you have a general idea of what is to be included in the Strategic Business Plan, let's go through the entire planning process. Because there are other critical activities taking place within the company that you cannot place in limbo during the strategic planning process, you should allocate plenty of calendar time between events. If you have only a handful of employees, you may be able to complete the task within one or two months; however, if you have a company with several hundred employees, six or seven months might be a more realistic time frame for completing the entire process. In my example, the strategic planning process is completed in thirty weeks, or slightly more than seven months (see Figure 10-1).

Figure 10-1. Typical timetable for SBP milestones.

Milestones	Timing (weeks prior to completion)
1: Strategic planning process kickoff meeting (led by CEO) (followed by development of 5-year sales projections)	30 weeks prior
2: Five-year sales projections briefing to VPs and SBP manager (led by team leaders) (followed by development of team-level briefing charts)	25 weeks prior
3: First-round team briefings to senior managers (led by team leaders)	21 weeks prior
4: Briefing of first-round results to CEO (by SBP manager and VPs)	20 weeks prior
5: Second-round team briefings to senior managers (led by team leaders)	17 weeks prior
6: Preliminary company SBP briefing to VPs (led by SBP manager)	9 weeks prior
7: Initial company SBP briefing to CEO (led by SBP manager)	4 weeks prior
8: Final company SBP briefing to CEO (led by SBP manager)	Completion date

Let's assume your company's fiscal year is the calendar year. We'll designate X as the week of the year in which you want to complete your SBP process and have the final briefing (in the following example, X is the week of December 1). The content and timing of the steps and milestones involved might be as follows:

Milestone 1: SBP Kick-off Meeting—May 15 (X minus 30 weeks)

The kickoff meeting is held by the CEO and attended by the senior executives and functional managers who will be responsible for implementing the SBP and who will probably be involved in the developmental process (some of them may delegate this function to a subordinate). During this pep talk and the subsequent discussion, the CEO establishes the tone for the planning process. If you are the chief executive conducting the meeting, choose your words carefully.

The meeting should begin with a briefing by the CEO that establishes an overall theme for the SBP process. The theme might be one of conservative expansion of existing products or perhaps bold initiatives involving new products and markets. Whatever theme you choose, it should be compatible with the company vision statement you developed in Step Nine. Encourage feedback from your executives and managers regarding additions or modifications to your vision statement.

In this meeting, outline your expectations in terms of growth and returns for the next five years, along with any specific baseline planning assumptions you wish the planning team to make.

Also announce the appointment of a senior member of your marketing team as the SBP manager (preselected by you). This person will be responsible for coordinating and managing the entire planning process.[5]

During the meeting, you and the SBP manager should establish a series of strategic planning teams—usually one team for each business segment—and designate leaders for each team. The teams should be interdisciplinary, consisting of representatives from engineering, operations, manufacturing, and other functional areas. Each team leader reports to the SBP manager.

You may want to suggest success goals for each business segment as a starting point for each planning team. You should discuss what you

---

5. The SBP manager is not necessarily the senior marketing executive, but may be a junior executive being groomed for more responsibility. Consideration should be given to rotating this position for future SBPs to allow different managers this leadership experience and challenge.

believe to be the company's top programs, products, and markets, as well as other anticipated initiatives during the next five years.

Before ending the meeting, present a schedule for the SBP process (as was shown in Figure 10-1). After the meeting is concluded, distribute a memo to all attendees that includes a written summary of your presentation, a timetable for completion of the SBP process, planning team rosters, and a listing of the success goals for each team.

Development of Five-Year Sales Projections

Following the kick-off meeting, the marketing members of each team prepare initial drafts of five-year sales projections, which will later be reviewed and finalized with the rest of the team members.

A typical five-year sales projections chart is shown in Figure 10-2.

Many businesses prepare overly optimistic sales projections that assume the company will win every order it pursues. These projections are rarely met; fate intervenes, and some of the expected orders don't materialize. Your SBP must account for such contingencies, and it will if you apply a probability factor.

Look at each full-value customer sale in Figure 10-2. Assign a percentage to each sale that represents the probability of the order being

Figure 10-2. Five-year sales projections (full value).

	FY94	FY95	FY96	FY97	FY98
Product Line #1					
Customer A Sales*	$280,000	$ 310,000	$ 330,000	$ 340,000	$ 350,000
Customer B Sales	160,000	190,000	220,000	250,000	280,000
Customer C Sales	90,000	110,000	130,000	150,000	170,000
Customer D Sales	0	80,000	160,000	240,000	320,000
Product Line #2					
Customer A Sales*	$ 0	$ 180,000	$ 180,000	$ 0	$ 0
Customer D Sales	170,000	230,000	250,000	270,000	290,000
Customer E Sales	0	150,000	180,000	210,000	240,000
Product Line #3					
Customer B Sales	$ 50,000	$ 100,000	$ 160,000	$ 220,000	$ 280,000
Customer F Sales	40,000	80,000	120,000	160,000	210,000
Customer G Sales	0	60,000	110,000	160,000	190,000
Totals	$790,000	$1,490,000	$1,840,000	$2,000,000	$2,330,000

*Some programs may involve more than one product line.

received. This is the sale's probability factor. A factor of 50 percent means that you have only a 50/50 chance of winning that particular order.

The effect of applying probability factors to the sales projections chart shown in Figure 10-2 is shown in Figure 10-3. (Figure 10-3 appears earlier in this chapter as Chart 10.)

Note that the factored projections are lower—and considerably more realistic—than the full-value projections. Your financiers will appreciate this fact and will more readily accept your projections because you will have already qualified them.

The Bottom Line

Now take one last look at the total dollar amount of sales you projected for the coming year on your factored sales projections chart. Do you have a gut feeling it is too large, that you have not accounted for everything that might go wrong? Or perhaps you believe it is too small; maybe you're not sure you've identified all of the potential near-term opportunities and believe that you should strive for additional sales.

Both of these situations require adding one more line to the chart for your first-year projections (FY94 in this example). If you believe sales are

Figure 10-3. Five-year sales projections (factored).

		FY94	FY95	FY96	FY97	FY98
Product Line #1	Factor (%)					
Customer A Sales*	80	$224,000	$ 248,000	$ 264,000	$ 272,000	$ 280,000
Customer B Sales	60	96,000	114,000	132,000	150,000	168,000
Customer C Sales	50	45,000	55,000	65,000	75,000	85,000
Customer D Sales	70	0	56,000	112,000	168,000	224,000
Product Line #2						
Customer A Sales*	50%	$ 0	$ 90,000	$ 90,000	$ 0	$ 0
Customer D Sales	80	136,000	184,000	200,000	216,000	232,000
Customer E Sales	60	0	90,000	108,000	126,000	144,000
Product Line #3						
Customer B Sales	70%	$ 35,000	$ 70,000	$ 112,000	$ 154,000	$ 196,000
Customer F Sales	80	32,000	64,000	96,000	128,000	168,000
Customer G Sales	70	0	42,000	77,000	112,000	133,000
Totals		$568,000	$1,013,000	$1,256,000	$1,401,000	$1,630,000

*Some programs may involve more than one product line.

understated, add a category called TASK. This represents the additional dollar value of sales you believe you can reasonably expect to achieve by working harder to secure orders. If you believe sales are overstated, add a category called DISCOUNT. This represents a negative dollar value that is added to from your projections to make them more realistic (see Figure 10-4).

Why go through this extra step? No matter how logically you calculated your factored sales projections, if your banker, managers, and/or board of directors believe the end result is overly pessimistic or overly optimistic, you'll have a hard time securing their commitment (financial or otherwise) to your company's five-year plan. This final "gut check" helps ensure that you will win the support of all of the key players who have some role in seeing that the plan is implemented.

Figure 10-4. Adding a task or a discount.

Section A. Bottom of unchanged five-year sales chart.

Customer F Sales	80% $ 32,000	$ 64,000	$ 96,000	$ 128,000	$ 168,000
Customer G Sales	70 0	42,000	77,000	112,000	133,000
Totals	$568,000	$1,013,000	$1,256,000	$1,401,000	$1,630,000

Section B. Bottom of five-year sales chart with a TASK added.

Customer F Sales	80% $ 32,000	$ 64,000	$ 96,000	$ 128,000	$ 168,000
Customer G Sales	70 0	42,000	77,000	112,000	133,000
Task	100,000				
Totals	$668,000	$1,013,000	$1,256,000	$1,401,000	$1,630,000

Section C. Bottom of five-year sales chart with a DISCOUNT added.

Customer F Sales	80% $ 32,000	$ 64,000	$ 96,000	$ 128,000	$ 168,000
Customer G Sales	70 0	42,000	77,000	112,000	133,000
Discount	(100,000)				
Totals	$468,000	$1,013,000	$1,256,000	$1,401,000	$1,630,000

Once you have added a task or a discount to your first-year projections, prepare a separate, detailed chart, further breaking down first-year sales by month. These data will be utilized throughout the year for comparing actual sales against the plan (some companies also prepare a sales breakdown by quarter for the following one or two years to help spot potential periods of very low or very high sales).

Milestone 2: Five-Year Sales Projections Briefing—June 15 (X minus 25 weeks)

Once the five-year sales projections have been developed, the planning team leaders brief the company's senior vice presidents and the SBP manager on their individual results, and the vice presidents give the teams further guidance for the next step by recommending changes to the numbers, the risk factors, or the other assumptions.

Development of Team-Level Briefing Charts

Following the sales projections briefing and feedback, each planning team develops its own set of first-round briefing charts for its particular business segment, to include the following elements:

- A restatement of success goals for the business segment and the market environment
- A characterization of the business segment and product portfolio (including strengths and weaknesses)
- An assessment of business segment competitors, as well as the competitive posture of the business segment's products
- Statements of objectives, strategies, and tactics[6] for the business segment (these will later be consolidated into company objectives)
- A factored sales projections summary for the next five years (broken down by major program and fiscal year)
- A summary statement of risks and opportunities that may affect projected sales figures for the coming year
- A summary of key issues for the business segment

---

6. As mentioned in a previous footnote, these are no longer "marketing" objectives, strategies, and tactics to secure orders, but rather "business segment" objectives, strategies, and tactics to ensure maximum profitability for the business segment.

(*Note*: After the second-round team briefing, these elements will be combined into the companywide SBP, in a format similar to that shown in the section "A Typical SBP" earlier in this chapter.)

Milestone 3: First-Round Team Briefings to Senior Managers—July 15 (X minus 21 weeks)

The teams present their first-round briefing charts to senior vice presidents and the SBP manager, for their review and comment. The vice presidents and the SBP manager point out strong and weak points of each presentation and direct each team to make needed improvements.

Milestone 4: Briefing of First-Round Planning Results to CEO—July 20 (X minus 20 weeks)

Following the first-round team briefings (Milestone 3), some important decisions need to be made by the senior executives and the SBP manager in concert with the CEO. A meeting is held at which the SBP manager and senior VPs give the CEO a progress report and address all concerns. In all probability, at this point there are too many strategies, requiring too many dollars to implement, and cuts or scalebacks are necessary.

In scaling back the team plans, senior management must consider a variety of questions, such as:

- What business are we in?
- What business should we be in, now and in the future?
- What is our distinctive competence today?
- Should we diversify/expand or prune/consolidate?
- What is the Return on Equity (ROE) and Return on Assets (ROA) of our various alternatives?

The management team should look at each product's position on the Growth-Share Matrix (see Appendix D) to ascertain which products should receive priority in terms of available resources.

As a result of this mid-term review, senior management must make strategic decisions on budgets, projects, and the potential emphasis on or elimination of products. The SBP manager must communicate this information back to the various strategic planning teams so that they can make appropriate adjustments.

Milestone 5: Second-Round Team Briefings to Senior Managers—August 15 (X minus 17 weeks)

Once the changes have been incorporated in each strategic planning team's briefing charts, they are once again presented to senior vice presidents and to the SBP manager. If any additional changes must be made, new charts should be provided to the SBP manager as soon as possible following the meeting.

Milestone 6: Preliminary Company SBP Briefing to VPs—October 1 (X minus 9 weeks)

Following the second-round briefing, the SBP manager takes all of the individual business segment briefings and—with the help of individual team leaders—begins the process of consolidating the material into a concise company briefing.

The SBP manager presents this first cut of the consolidated briefing charts to senior vice presidents for their final recommendations, then works with team leaders to implement additional changes if required. Whether or not changes are needed, the SBP manager should meet with representatives of each business segment to show them the plan that will be presented to the chief executive.

Milestone 7: Initial Company SBP Briefing to CEO—November 1 (X minus 4 weeks)

Now it's time for the SBP manager to present the initial set of consolidated SBP charts to the CEO, with vice presidents and team leaders on hand to support the presentation and to answer any questions the CEO may have. As a result of this presentation, there may be some additional modifications to the plan. The SBP manager should work with the vice presidents and team leaders to implement these changes.

Milestone 8: Final Company SBP Briefing to CEO—December 1 (Week X)

Four weeks after the initial company SBP briefing, the SBP manager conducts a final SBP briefing with the CEO, with vice presidents in attendance. If any minor changes to the SBP are still required, the CEO should work directly with the SBP manager to ensure these are made in the document. Then the chief executive should send a memorandum of thanks to all team members for their efforts.

A Word of Caution

The completed SBP is your company's business bible. This vital document should be treated as company confidential material. After the process is complete, copies of the Strategic Business Plan should be prepared for limited distribution to vice presidents only. Even though copies are closely guarded, all managers must have access to the SBP when necessary. But managers who want to refer to the plan should secure it from their respective vice presidents; additional copies should not be made.

Implementation

Putting your Strategic Business Plan on paper is one thing; seeing that it's implemented is quite another. The SBP process outlined in this chapter overcomes the most serious potential implementation problem—the failure of the CEO, managers, and employees to embrace the plan—by having all key players involved throughout the process. This involvement gives them a true feeling of ownership.

Beyond the commitment of key players, effective implementation means that:

- A specific time frame has been assigned to each key task outlined in the SBP charts.
- A specific person has been assigned the responsibility of carrying out each key task.
- A briefing structure has been established to ensure that the CEO and appropriate senior management are kept apprised of the progress of the plan.
- Monthly sales figures are extracted from the financials and circulated to key management so that they can compare these actual figures with the detailed monthly sales projections developed in the SBP.

EXERCISE: A Vision for Your SBP Kickoff

Now that you understand the SBP Process, create a section in your notebook entitled "My SBP Kickoff." Contemplate a meaningful vision for your SBP process, whether it be a dynamic initiative to introduce new products, a bold thrust into new markets, or an orderly expansion of your existing lines. You set the tone and the stage for the theme and the goals, and remember they should not be at odds with your company vision statement. Finally, give some thought to the question of who your SBP manager should be. If you have a small company, it could well be you, but, as your company grows, pass the baton to another senior manager—I guarantee you'll be astonished with the results.

Epilogue
Ensuring the Annuity

It would be nice if all things remained constant. But economies peak and bottom out, distribution pipelines plug up, plentiful raw materials become scarce overnight, customers' needs change, and interest rates go on roller-coaster rides. In other words, one thing is certain: The business environment next year will be different than this year.

A Yearly Process

If you want to ensure that your business maximizes its true potential, you must commit to an annual renewal of your strategic planning effort. This involves far more than just going through the steps outlined in Step Ten alone; it requires going through every step in the Macrofruition process.

However, you will find that the first nine steps will require far less effort the second time around. When you return to each step the following year, you need only review progress, setbacks, and any modifications that must be made to keep your company prospering for another year. Then track these changes in your notebook.

The first steps in the annual review process should require minimal time and effort. However, when you reach Step Ten, the SBP process, you must always allow for the full scheduled period so that your strategic teams can achieve the best possible outcome.

Every year, after you've completed the SBP process, consider inviting your banker and/or other financial backers to a sanitized version of the SBP briefing that doesn't reveal any crucial strategies or proprietary information about new products or processes. Even though they won't have written copies, this briefing will impress upon your financial backers that your management team is committed to success, making them more likely to loosen their purse strings.

It's also a good idea to brief your board of directors each year as you complete the planning process. Not only is it important to keep them informed about the progress and plans for the company, it's wise to solicit their input as interested and well-informed outsiders.

As you focus on achieving your business goals with the help of the Macrofruition process, don't forget to focus some of your energies on *enjoying* your accomplishments. For when you finally step down from the helm and pass the reins of leadership to the next generation, you'll look back on the journey—not its conclusion—as the best time of your life.

Appendix A
Suggested Readings in Total Quality Management

The following books are recommended as excellent resources to study as you move toward implementing your own Total Quality Management (TQM) program:

- Brocka, Bruce, and Suzanne Brocka. *Quality Management: Implementing the Best Ideas of the Masters.* New York: Business One-Irwin, 1992.
- The Ernst & Young Quality Improvement Consulting Group. *Total Quality: An Executive's Guide for the 1990s.* Homewood, IL: Dow Jones-Irwin, 1990.
- Hunt, V. Daniel. *Quality in America: How to Implement a Competitive Quality Program.* New York: Business One-Irwin, 1992.
- Jablonski, Joseph. *Implementing TQM: Competing in the Nineties Through Total Quality Management, Second Edition.* Albuquerque, NM: Technical Management Consortium, 1992.
- Russell, J. P. *The Quality Master Plan.* Milwaukee: ASQC Quality Press, 1990.

Appendix B
Competitive Analysis

The following document is a representative competitive analysis (adapted from a real analysis with the company/staff identities changed). Take note of how much more you would know about this company in an actual competitive situation after developing this document.

ACME Corporation Executive Summary

The ACME Corporation (hereinafter referred to as ACME) is in the business of the design, development, manufacture, and support of home satellite dishes. ACME systems include antennas, digital communications receivers, and satellite tracking and control systems. The corporation qualifies as a small business and posted sales of $32.3 million for Fiscal Year 1993, ending March 31, 1993.

ACME has been involved with satellite TV reception since 1982, starting with systems analysis and studies. It is perceived as a good study house, with the ability to produce small-quantity, specialized equipment. In order to achieve its 1994 sales goal of $60 million, ACME will try to establish a production capability and find commercial, government, niche, and international markets for its products.

ACME Corporate Perspective

ACME was incorporated in Arizona on May 1, 1981. It was founded by three staff members from Ford Aerospace and Communications Corporation: James Brown, John Acres, and Marshall Forrest (Acres and Forrest remain as consultants and board members only). Growth through the 1980s was through system studies and consulting work for NASA, private industry development contracts, and hardware development of the company's own line of products.

The three founders continue to occupy key positions within the corporation and have been joined by well-respected senior managers (see Figure B-1). The technical nature of the ACME upper management is reflected in the character and personality of the corporation.

Note in Figure B-2 that the officers are all in the 45-to-55 age bracket. Within the next five to eight years, the ACME upper management corps will be approaching retirement age. Figure B-3 lists the members of ACME's board of directors and its standing committees.

Figure B-1. ACME executive organization chart.

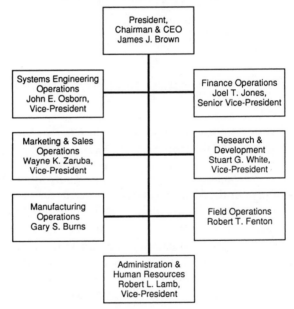

Figure B-2. Company officers and ages.

Title	Officer	Age
President, Chairman & CEO	Dr. James J. Brown	51
Senior Vice-President & CFO	Joel T. Jones	48
Vice-President	John E. Osborn	45
Vice-President	Wayne K. Zaruba	54
Vice-President	Robert L. Lamb	55
Vice-President	Stuart G. White	49

Figure B-3. ACME board of directors and committees.

Board of Directors

Chairman	Dr. James J. Brown
Consultant & Co-Founder	John W. Acres
Consultant & Co-Founder	Dr. Marshal Forrest
Senior Vice-President	Joel T. Jones
Vice-President	John E. Osborn
Managing Partner (Technology Ventures)	Dr. Albert J. Perry
Chairman & CEO (California Satellite Systems, Inc.)	Dr. David Larson

Standing Board Committees

Compensation:	Brown, Forrest, Larson, and Perry
Audit:	Forrest, Larson, and Perry
Stock Plans:	Forrest, Larson, and Perry

ACME Marketing Organization

ACME is organized into the following market divisions under Vice President Wayne Zaruba:

- *Consumer Products Division*, managed by Peter Hobbs. This division markets to the general consumer market throughout the United States, using both in-house marketing staff and field office staff (field staff offices are managed by Robert Fenton).

- *Industrial Products Division*, managed by Jamie Waters. This division focuses on selling to cable networks and to commercial and public networks and stations throughout the United States, using a smaller in-house marketing staff, as well as the field staff.

- *Government/International Products Division*, managed by Matthew Rogers. This division focuses on contracts with the U.S. Government and with international agencies.

- *Advanced Programs Department*, managed by Jeremy Helms. This is a two-person shop that focuses on future satellite product needs for the telecommunications industry.

The following is a brief summary of the product focus of the four marketing divisions:

■ *Consumer Products Division.* This division's primary product is a moderately priced satellite receiver, the "Cat's Eye" Model 220. The unit is capable of receiving all commercial satellite signals in use today and has available a popular option that incorporates all the required decoding electronics for subscription services (HBO, Showtime, Cinemax, etc.) at a substantial savings over separate decoders.

■ *Industrial Products Division.* This division's primary product is the new Time Division Multiple Access (TDMA) satellite communications equipment for broadcast operations (Model 1105). It is rumored the division is about to announce a new version, Model 2210, that will have double the older model's capacity.

■ *Government/International Products Division.* This division's primary product focus is on a new GRS (Ground Receiver System) to receive and process data from the MILSTAR Satellite Network. It is rumored that ACME has designed a new model of antijam communications receiver for the U.S. Air Force SATCOM satellite communications system. This division also markets the consumer and industrial divisions' products internationally.

■ *Advanced Programs Department.* This department is known to be working on a satellite tracking system for commercial vehicles, including trains, trucks, and buses. The department is also competing for a NASA study contract that would track all satellites and space debris in orbit about the earth for a classified program to eliminate this space-flight hazard.

Financial Highlights

ACME has shown good increases in sales and net worth over previous years, and a continuation of this upward trend is expected. Figure B-4 shows the company's recent financial performance. ACME's first major win was a 1986 $2.5 million U.S. Air Force SAMSO (Space and Missile Systems Organization) contract for design, development, fabrication, and support of equipment that receives and relays satellite messages among units of the U.S. armed forces throughout the world. ACME was able to get the program designated as a small-business set-aside and thereby eliminate major competitors.

The first public offering of 1 million shares of common stock was made in October 1991. The offering was motivated by the recognition that further growth required additional working capital. The net proceeds

Figure B-4. ACME financial performance.

Year Ending	Sales ($ Million)	Net Worth ($ Million)
March 31, 1983 (1983 was founding year)	0.4	0.03
March 31, 1990	11.1	1.7
March 31, 1991	15.6	2.6
December 31, 1991 (public offering of 1 million shares of common stock)		13.4
March 31, 1992	23.2	14.2
March 31, 1993	32.3	16.8
March 31, 1994 (forecast)	60.0	

Sales Breakdown:	Consumer	44%
	Industrial	34
	Government	18
	International	4

were used largely to supplement working capital, with some capital expenditures and debt reduction also covered. As a result, ACME's working capital is cash-centered and exceeds $10 million. The company's debt is light compared to net worth, and the overall financial condition is good.

With 3,500,000 shares outstanding, 69 percent of capital stock is owned by the officers and directors and 15 percent is controlled by the chairman.

ACME's outstanding growth record—with annual sales and earnings advancing 41 percent and 56 percent respectively for the last five years—should continue. ACME's latest annual report indicates order bookings of $52 million in FY 1993. The company's returns are modest, with ROS of 11 percent at its peak and ROA declining over the FY93 period from 24 percent to 16 percent, both the result of ACME's significant reliance on the industrial and government business sectors, which are softening.

Facilities

ACME's home office is in Phoenix, Arizona. In 1992, the company expanded its leased space from 65,000 square feet to 83,000, with plans for additional expansion into the entire 100,000 square feet of its present two-story building. ACME operates an engineering and R&D facility in McLean, Virginia (closer to government and industrial customers), in a 14,100-square-foot leased facility.

Work Force

Total employment is about 400, with about 320 of the personnel located at the Phoenix facility. It is believed that the actual in-plant technical work force is closer to 600, because of ACME's practice of contracting for labor, particularly for specialized communications consultants (two prominent ACME consultants are Dr. Brad Peters and Dr. Don Grant, both preeminent scientists in the satellite communications field).

Of the 400 full-time employees, 68 percent are in technical operations and 14 percent are engaged in manufacturing in a nonunion environment. Virtually all employees are covered by a two-part retirement plan. The company contributes to a pension plan and a profit-sharing plan; starting in FY 1993, employees can make voluntary before-tax salary deferral contributions to the profit-sharing plan. In addition, ACME has a cash bonus plan covering almost all employees that is based on a percent of operating profits. ACME provided approximately $410,000 in FY 1993 to this cash bonus plan. Employees are well compensated and have added monetary incentive through the cash bonus plan to see that ACME is profitable.

The skilled labor turnover rate has averaged less than 5 percent over recent years, whereas a 30 percent turnover in nonskilled jobs is common for the industry. In summary, the ACME skilled personnel are highly competent technically and motivated financially and have challenging front-end systems and design tasks; however, they have limited upward mobility within the organization because of the small number of management levels.

(Insert financial report highlights from last annual report here.)

Manufacturing Capability

ACME has a very limited manufacturing capability. The company's product base is characterized as limited-quantity, special-purpose, laboratory- or commercial-grade equipment. The manufacturing process at ACME is labor-intensive and involves significant subcontract activity. Machining, circuit-board manufacturing, environmental testing, and other tasks beyond ACME's in-house capabilities are done by subcontractors performing to ACME plans and specifications. ACME is currently emphasizing improved manufacturing quality and cost performance. In FY 1993 the company invested $6.9 million in the plant and in capital equipment, up 65 percent from FY 1992. ACME added a computer-aided design system with an automated Hewlett-Packard test system, which permits testing of every component on a PC board within thirty seconds. To assist in the assembly of cables, a computer-driven cable tester was procured.

Notice that this equipment helps ACME continue to accomplish what the company already does, but in a more efficient manner, as opposed to adding new manufacturing capability. ACME has been hesitant in the past to expend significant working capital at one time to achieve in-house manufacturing capability (focusing instead on ensuring that its employees remain adequately compensated) and will probably retain this philosophy. Therefore, significant manufacturing capability is expected to be developed in several stages consistent with an overall growth plan.

Acquisition Potential

ACME appears to be a viable acquisition candidate for companies that have a complementary business focus. Company strengths can be summarized as: (1) strong upper management, (2) recognized technical competence, (3) outstanding financial performance, and (4) narrow but strong U.S. DOD presence. Because 69 percent of the outstanding shares of stock are owned by the officers and directors, sale of the company will take a very attractive offer by a suitor and a consensus by ACME management. Because the corporate direction and decision-making power lies primarily with Dr. Brown, it is clear that he is the key.

It is believed that ACME's growth strategy is to merge into a large corporation (this will be discussed under "Objectives and Strategies").

The ideal suitor would be seeking to enter the market addressed by ACME, would have an established high-volume production capability, and would need help with design and development.

Products and Markets

ACME's product base can be partitioned into four groups:

1. Relatively inexpensive consumer-grade satellite receivers (typical price of Model 220: $2,200)
2. Moderately expensive industrial satellite receiver equipment utilizing the latest time-division multiple-access technology (typical price of Model 1105: $17,500; of Model 2210: $24,000 est.)
3. Custom-designed government products, primarily for military satellite network communications (typical price: $150,000 est.)
4. Advanced program R&D efforts (typical contract: $2–$5 million)

Perhaps more significant than the product equipment base, in terms of capabilities and future market presence, is the large number of R&D and development contracts that ACME has won over the last eleven years. These contracts cover almost every aspect of satellite communications and configurations involving regional and global coverage under poor signal strength conditions.

As a result of these contracts, ACME has the technical expertise to address a wide range of new products and markets. ACME's consumer product Model 220 combines both the receiver and the encryption decoder in a single cost-effective package. It is an excellent value, although it has a "worse-than-average" quality rating—the result of being fabricated by a series of subcontract assembly houses.

Similarly, the company's industrial products—Models 1105 and 2210—enjoy a fine reputation for capability but are plagued with quality problems as well. Only in the Government Products Division—which involves low-volume equipment, always designed and built in-house—does quality not seem to be a problem.

A significant portion of ACME's growth during the past five years has occurred in the government sector. Indeed, the company's latest annual report does not mention any significant new technology breakthroughs in the consumer market. With the recent cutbacks in government budgets, ACME's growth curve could flatten out without a significant new strategic thrust.

Objectives and Strategies

In order to achieve its 1994 sales goal of $60 million, ACME will need to expand its business base significantly into international markets. The company will have to develop some semblance of a production capability in order to be able to compete on programs involving even moderate production quantities.

Here are some potential objectives and strategies for ACME:

Objective: *Develop a production capability.*
Strategies: 1. Funnel working capital into manufacturing equipment or facilities.
              2. Continue to win low-volume production programs.
              3. Offer other volume manufacturers ACME's technology insertion on a royalty basis.
Objective: *Initiate a major expansion into international markets.*
Strategies: 1. Adapt and market existing commercial and industrial designs to the European and Pacific Rim communities.
              2. Establish partnership(s) with select international trading companies.
              3. Develop major PR campaign focusing on key printed media in the targeted international markets.
Objective: *Expand into embryonic new markets where sophisticated communications/data transfer systems are required.*
Strategies: 1. Form strategic alliances with other companies in the development of targeted products.
              2. Focus on the design phase and choose partners with major manufacturing capability for the near term.
              3. Evolve own product line as significant production capacity is realized.

It is rumored that ACME and Motorola are jointly developing an integrated communications and data reference system aimed at airline and business aircraft markets, a system that would be marketed by Motorola.

ACME will continue to look for opportunities to get government procurement agencies to set aside programs for small businesses. However, ACME is moving away from a small-business mentality.

In the 1980s most of ACME's business was R&D-oriented, but today it is resource-dominated by development, manufacture, and support activities. ACME has not forsaken R&D, but is has wisely formulated a more traditional large-business balance.

Management's goal of $60 million in sales by 1994 shows that ACME is planning to outgrow its small-business image. The directors plan to continue to build a solid management team and competent, skilled staff.

ACME's outstanding performance and prospects for continued growth make it a prime candidate for acquisition. As discussed earlier, acquisition will require agreement by the officers and board of directors, who own 69 percent of the common stock.

Within four years, when CEO/Chairman Brown reaches fifty-five years of age, he (and possibly other senior executives) will want to cash out, so it is likely that ACME will merge or be acquired.

In the meantime, ACME will try to ensure that it is an attractive acquisition. Given that Dr. Larson is the CEO of California Satellite Systems, Inc., which has complementary business interests, and is on the ACME board of directors, it is reasonable to expect a merger of these companies.

ACME has a number of competitive strengths. As a small business, it is able to focus resources and to redirect them quickly. The decision power resides with a few key people, Brown and the officers, and, because there are only a few tiers of management, decision points are reached quickly. ACME has a strong technical reputation within the satellite communications community, and its low skilled labor turnover rate provides continuity. ACME's public offering of common stock has provided the company with a relatively large working capital base from which management intends to support expansion.

The small-business nature of ACME means that it has competitive shortcomings as well. The company does not possess the necessary resources to pursue major government programs as a prime contractor. The marketing staff lacks significant national visibility, and the company is virtually unknown outside of its core markets. However, ACME's marketing team is able effectively to focus its efforts very narrowly when the program is key to its plans. ACME staff works around the company's limited production capability but would have trouble being cost-competitive on programs with large production content. It may make sense for ACME to design future communications hardware entirely for manufacturing and marketing by other major communications corporations (as it is rumored to be doing with Motorola).

Conclusions

Organization. For the near term, ACME should continue to experience moderate growth and stability.

Financial. ACME will continue to achieve outstanding sales, orders, and net worth performance. The company has a good business base, with good growth opportunities. Its product portfolio offers major growth opportunities, provided the company can effectively address its manufacturing capability shortfall.

Products. ACME's technological expertise has led to a first-class, relatively broad (consumer, industrial, and government) product line. Provided the company can overcome quality problems derived from the current necessity to subcontract a high percentage of manufacturing, the product line should continue to evolve into top-of-the-line systems for the satellite communications industry.

Markets. ACME wants to play with the big boys. The company has attempted to win major programs and has thus far been unsuccessful. However, it is learning to become a formidable adversary. At the same time, the company has not shown a significant marketing presence and must remedy that situation in order to be successful on big programs.

Acquisition Potential. It is very likely that ACME will be acquired by a larger company in the field within the next five years.

Appendix C

Competitive Briefing Charts

Following is a typical set of competitive briefing charts. The purpose of the charts is to present a brief overview of the primary competition to senior management. In this example, the company—APEX Corporation—is in the business of marketing a highly successful driveway alarm system for vehicles, dubbed "Sentinel."

The charts include an analysis of APEX's top four competitors: Alpha, Beta, Delta, and Sigma. In your own analysis, you might consider including a fifth company—your own—to show how your company compares to the competition.

Top Four Competitors

(Chart 1)

Competitive Environment

- Our company's product, SENTINEL, has captured 40 percent of the vehicle detection market and has become the industry standard on which all competitive systems are based.
- The market size is increasing at 20 percent per year, so there is additional market share to be gained by all competitors.
- Competitors are focusing on "leapfrogging" our technology to arrive at a new generation of products.
- The emphasis in the marketplace is to reduce the cost of the detection systems.
- Competitors will seek out and develop nontraditional niche markets to erode our position.

(Chart 2)

Competitive Comparisons—Latest Fiscal Year

	Company ALPHA	Company BETA	Company DELTA	Company SIGMA
Volume of competitive product sales	$5.1MM	$17.2MM	$4.3MM	$6.5MM
Total company sales volume	$32.4MM	$240.0MM	$154.0MM	$102.0MM
Product staffing	50 people	85 people	65 people	55 people
Organization capabilities	Strong & stable	Retrenching	Merger: Loss of autonomy	New people & new facility
Company characteristics	Strong analytically	Heavy spenders	Aggressive technology marketing	Relying on past product technologies
Product capabilities	Limited, small volume	Gearing up to high volume	High volume	Limited volume
Perceived ability to meet customer requirements	Good on development; poor on products	Demands the customer accept their solution	Very accommodating to customer requirements	Strong with proposals; performance shaky

(Chart 3)

Security Product Business Base

Alpha

- Home Burglar Alarms ($10MM)
- Electric-Eye Systems ($8MM)

Beta

- Industrial Security Systems ($45MM)
- Laser Beam Sensors ($30MM)

Delta

- Industrial Surveillance Systems ($38MM)
- Metal Detectors ($20MM)

Sigma

- Commercial Traffic Control Systems ($60MM)
- Buried Coil Vehicle Sensors ($10MM)

(Chart 4)

Key Objectives and Strategies

Alpha

- Leverage burglar alarm system knowledge into next-generation system to attack industrial markets.
- Utilize latest technology to update electric eye into new product for commercial markets.
- Posture company as attractive acquisition candidate.

Beta

- Concentrate on expanding core industrial security products business.
- Couple laser sensor technology into major new commercial detection system.
- Avoid head-on sensor competition unless it yields technology advance.

Delta

- Adapt surveillance systems for international requirements and markets.
- Pursue and win military surveillance systems development programs.
- Redesign metal detector into next-generation system utilizing space-program magnetometer.

Sigma

- Create next-generation traffic control and detection system.
- Expand with improved buried coil sensor into commercial niche markets.
- Evolve industrial coil sensor into a vehicle driveway alarm system for unsealed consumer driveways.

(Chart 5)

Key Issues

Alpha

- Enhance power to compete with larger, better capitalized competitors.
- Overcome reputation for poor product quality.
- Raise funds for capital investment for manufacturing expansion.

Beta

- Sales have leveled off; needs more profitable growth to fuel planned new products.
- Must soften belligerent, arrogant attitude and focus on customer service.
- Lacks ability to spend resources for major new design without achieving customer acceptance first.

Delta

- Maintain growth and drive despite new parent company management.
- Achieve significant product growth in market in which it has done poorly.
- Negotiate exclusive access to NASA detector circuit for new product line.

Sigma

- Overcome growing inability to win major new customers.
- Rebuild management capability following reorganization.
- Adapt obsolete technology into products the marketplace will want.

(Chart 6)

(A competitive ranking of all companies, including yours, would be inserted here, as computed from an analysis similar to Figure 8-1.)

Appendix D

The Growth-Share Matrix

The Growth-Share Matrix originated with the Boston Consulting Group (BCG) in the early 1970s. This simple 2 x 2 matrix (Figure D-1) divides products (or business segments) into four categories: Stars, Cash Cows, Question Marks, and Dogs.

1. *Stars.* Stars are the high-growth, high-market-share products. Examples include personal computers, CD players, and VCRs in their early years.

Stars generate significant amounts of cash because of the volume of business they generate. They also require the expenditure of large amounts of cash in order to maintain their rapid growth rates.

The growth rate of stars generally tapers off over time. A typical Star strategy is to invest as necessary to maintain this business segment's market leadership.

2. *Cash Cows.* If market share remains high but growth tapers off, a Star becomes a Cash Cow. These are products that have maintained their market leadership even as growth has tapered off, thus reaping the rewards from previous investment in making them leaders. These products are inexpensive to maintain but they generate high profits. Examples of Cash Cows include Life-Savers, Bic ballpoint pens, and Hershey chocolate bars.

The usual Cash Cow strategy is to reinvest only enough to maintain the product's current position, then use the excess cash to invest in other projects.

3. *Question Marks.* Question marks are high-growth, low-market-share products. With sufficient cash and innovative marketing, they might become Stars, but if either of these ingredients is lacking, they may

Figure D-1. The BCG growth-share matrix concept.

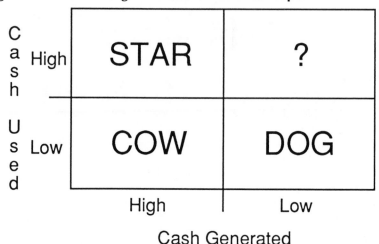

become Dogs (described below). Examples of current Question Marks include solar-powered vehicles, TV phones, pen personal computers, and interactive TV.

When it comes to strategy, you probably can't afford to finance all of your Question Marks adequately; instead, you should select the most promising few, fund them to the maximum, and eliminate the rest.

4. *Dogs.* If market share drops, a Star may become a Dog. A Dog is a slow-growth, low-market-share product that neither requires nor generates significant amounts of cash. Past examples include the Edsel automobile, 3-D movies, and eight-track audio cartridges.

Unless they offer some unique strategic advantage or generate significantly more cash than they use, the best strategy is to divest your company of these products or identify new, more profitable market niches.

Your company's overall strategy should be to strive for a healthy balance in your product portfolio. You need some Stars (to mature into tomorrow's Cash Cows). You need as many Cash Cows as possible, because they provide the money to finance other business areas. You must separate the vital few Question Marks from the trivial many, because you cannot afford to fund every opportunity well. And if you have any Dogs, you'd best get rid of them.

It's a good idea to examine your product portfolio annually and compare it to portfolios of years past to ensure that it is adapting to the changing needs of the marketplace.

Index